BARBARA ANN SCOTT

Queen of the Ice

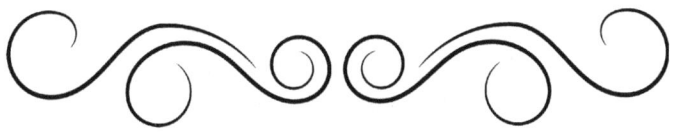

Ryan Stevens

Canadian Cataloguing in Publication Data

Title: Barbara Ann Scott: Queen of the Ice
Author: Stevens, Ryan, 1982-
ISBN: 9781069170521

Copyright © 2025
by Ryan Stevens

Independently published
All rights reserved

Every reasonable effort has been made to credit all source material included used in this book.

If errors or omissions have occurred, they will be corrected in future editions provided written notification and supporting documentation has been received by the author.

TABLE OF CONTENTS

Introduction	1
1	3
2	18
3	24
4	29
5	38
6	50
7	55
8	62
9	70
10	122
11	132
12	135
13	142
14	151
15	162
Appendix A – Firsts	170
Appendix B – Competitive Record	172
Appendix C – Tour Itinerary	174
Appendix D – Genealogy	178
Sources	182
Appreciation	192
Author's Note	194
Other Books	195

Barbara Ann Scott. Photo courtesy BAnQ: Bibliothèque et Archives nationales du Québec. Rights: Public domain.

Barbara Ann Scott. Photo courtesy BAnQ: Bibliothèque et Archives nationales du Québec. Rights: Public domain.

Barbara Ann Scott. Photo courtesy BAnQ: Bibliothèque et Archives nationales du Québec. Rights: Public domain.

INTRODUCTION

Writing a memorable biography is like choreographing a winning figure skating program. Both writers and choreographers need grace, fluidity and creativity. There's a lot of trial and error. Before anyone sees the finished work, authors and choreographers cut, change around and rework elements to improve the pace and flow. They must also pay close attention to the technical aspects. In skating, these are jumps, spins and lifts; in nonfiction writing, it means getting every fact and figure right.

If somebody else adapted Barbara Ann Scott's story to a film, her saccharine-sweet personality would all be a facade. Her mother would be portrayed as a controlling Mommie Dearest figure or a caricature of LaVona Harding. The plot would feature a bitter rivalry between Barbara Ann and Sonja Henie, climaxing in a scene where one of them throws a drink in the other's face. A jealous rival might even resort to sabotaging Barbara Ann's skates or scratching her record right before the Olympics. This is the sort of juicy story that fiction lovers go bonkers over, but none of this is true and that's not the kind of book I would ever want to write.

As you'll come to learn in the chapters that follow, Barbara Ann's life was marked by both challenges and triumphs, ultimately illustrating the timeless truth that sometimes "nice people finish first".

Before diving in, I want to share the same disclaimer that I have with my previous books:

This is a figure skating book written for figure skating people.

Not every book should cater to a general audience, and this one was written for the thousands of dedicated and knowledgeable figure skating fans around the world that "give a flutz" about the sport's history.

If that's you, you're going to find this book interesting. If facts and figures about figure skating bore you to tears, you're in the wrong place.

My dear skating lovers, I hope you enjoy reading about a Canadian skating legend. Most importantly, I hope you learn something new.

1

"In a slightly scary way, I sometimes feel as though I, Barbara Ann, didn't exist at all. I often seem to be something people have conjured up in their minds, something they want to believe I am, something a little bit better than perfect - which no one can be." - Barbara Ann Scott

Barbara Ann Scott was born May 9, 1928, on an unseasonably warm day in Canada's capital. She grew up in an ordinary Ottawa home, with an ordinary name, yet her family was far from ordinary.

Barbara Ann's father Clyde Rutherford Scott abandoned his studies in Mining Engineering at Queen's University to join the 42nd Lanark and Renfrew Regiment of the Canadian Expeditionary Force during The Great War.

Serving on the front lines during the Battle of Langemarck, Clyde faced a sudden ambush at a farmhouse. He sustained multiple injuries: rifle and machine gun fire wounds in both hips and one knee and shrapnel in his left eye. The severity of his injuries led the Germans to mistakenly believe that he had perished. They left him among a pile of dead bodies until a dog alerted them to his survival.

Major William Beattie, the Chaplain to the 1st Infantry Brigade, sent a telegram to the Mayor of Perth. The telegram falsely stated that Clyde had passed away.

Consequently, his parents held a memorial service in his honour.

Clyde spent over two years in German and Swiss Prisoner of War camps before being repatriated to England in 1917. His parents were shocked and delighted when he eventually made his way back to Canada on a hospital ship, but his injuries were so severe that he had to have nine surgeries upon his return to Ontario. Though permanently disabled, he earned the rank of Lieutenant-Colonel and the 1914-15 Star, British War Medal and Victory Medal. When Barbara Ann was born, he was serving as the military's Assistant Director of Records. He was later appointed Military Secretary of National Defence.

Clyde and Barbara Ann's mother, Mary Purvis Derbyshire, had not yet crossed paths. However, Mary faced tough times of her own while Clyde was interned in a series of POW Camps in Europe.

Soon after marrying William Chalmers MacLaren, Mary moved to the U.S. with her husband, daughter Mary, and son William to live the California dream. Mary's husband William was a Director of the Ottawa, Rideau Valley and Brockville Railway Company and a manufacturer of gloves and suspenders.

The marriage ended when Mary divorced her husband on the grounds of neglect and non-support. She supported herself by working as a real estate agent in San Francisco. Through her family's high-society connections, Mary was introduced to Clyde. They continued to correspond over time after their first introduction, and over time a relationship blossomed. They planned a quiet wedding in Boston. However, their wedding was delayed because Mary couldn't produce a divorce certificate from her first marriage. It was over a week before the necessary paperwork materialized. The couple married in 1927. They settled into a modest brick house at 648 Rideau Street in the Ottawa neighbourhood of Sandy Hill.

Mary's family was extremely prominent in her hometown of Brockville. Her great-grandfather was a Senator and Member of Parliament, Hon. Daniel Derbyshire. A popular dairy supplier, he was known as "The Eastern Ontario Cheese King". Her great uncle Hon. Robert Alfred Ernest Greenshields was Chief Justice of the Superior Court of the Province of Quebec. Justice Greenshields served as a defence lawyer in the trial of Louis Riel when he was arrested for his role in the Northwest Rebellion. Her godfather was Viscount Richard Bedford Bennett, who served as Canada's 11th Prime Minister from 1930 to 1935.

Barbara Ann was raised in a church-going Anglican family with conservative values. She was essentially an only child, as her half-siblings were considerably older than her. As divorce was a taboo subject at the time, Barbara Ann's half-sister Mary lived with the family briefly, but she was passed off as a servant. She married a hockey player in 1934 and moved to Brockville. Barbara Ann's half-brother William was sent off to be raised by his grandparents in Brockville when he was ten and was not really a presence in the household.

Barbara Ann's father Clyde gave her the childhood nickname Tinker - after Tinker Bell - the fairy from the book *Peter Pan*. He called her this because she was so small and dainty. He insisted Barbara Ann wear her hair quite short when she was young. Her mother put a ribbon on it so the neighbours would know she was a girl.

Barbara Ann regarded her father as "a wonderful man. He was kind but he was strict." Though fiercely independent, Clyde was unable to bend over and was plagued by the injuries he had suffered during The Great War.

"His body was full of shrapnel," Barbara Ann remembered. "He'd get a little red spot on his arm and it would fester and finally out would come a little piece of metal. This happened for years." Determined to be independent, he designed a pair of three-foot-long pincers, so he could pull on his socks and tie his shoelaces. He would limp his way through basketball games and rounds of golf at the Kingsmere Golf Club near the family's summer cottage. Clyde and Mary both valued modesty, kindness and hard work and tried to instill these values in Barbara Ann. They also both loved animals. The family home was overrun with a menagerie of pets, including two dogs, two rabbits, a cat, a canary, a family of mud turtles and a white rat. Visiting The Scotts was like visiting a miniature petting zoo.

When she was only three years old, Barbara Ann first expressed an interest in skating. She wrote a letter to Santa Claus, care of a local radio station, asking for a pair of "one-runner skates and a horse". When Santa brought her a pair of black skates with double runners, she was none too pleased. She thumped her bum down on frozen Dow's Lake to watch a man who was ice fishing while her mother skated nearby. She hated the double runners and never used them again, but her interest in skating never waned.

When Barbara Ann was five, and taking music lessons from former Olympic figure skater Fran Claudet, she said, "If I do my music well, will you ask my mother to let me skate?" Fran encouraged her to take up the sport and spoke to her parents about it. Santa finally brought her a 'real' pair of skates when she was six. Barbara Ann was taken over to skate on the crowded Junior sessions at the Minto Skating Club's rink on Waller Street, just east of where the Rideau Centre is today.

Melville Rogers, the first man to represent Canada at the Winter Olympic Games in 1924, was the biggest mover and shaker at the Minto Skating Club, so much so that he came to be known as "Mr. Minto". He recognized very early on that there was something special about Barbara Ann. At his suggestion, Barbara Ann was quickly moved up to the Intermediate session. There she was able to receive instruction from the club's professional at the time: Gustave Lussi. Unfortunately, she missed most of her first skating season, as she was quite sickly at the time. She had whooping cough and a series of mastoid operations when she was an infant and was plagued by ear problems throughout her young life. When her mother kept her home from the rink, she would take her skates to bed with her instead of her dolls.

Barbara Ann took her first figure test when she was seven. She weighed only fifty or sixty pounds at the time, and the judges had to get down on all fours to see her faint tracings on the ice. That winter, she performed in her first Minto Follies, dressed as a Käthe Kruse doll in a brown, yellow and white plaid dress, a white blouse and a big bow in her hair. *The Ottawa Citizen* raved, "Barbara Ann Scott, a little seven-year-old lady... literally stole the hearts of the audience with her daintiness and captivating solo in which she did front and back spirals and ballet jumps extraordinarily well for one so young."

Gustave Lussi left the Minto Skating Club not long after Barbara Ann's arrival. Paul Wilson took over as the Club's professional in 1935. The Swede was followed by two other European coaches, Rudolf Praznowski of Czechoslovakia and Freddy Mésot of Belgium. In those days, skaters took from whatever professional the club employed, and coach-hopping wasn't something that was typically done. Praznowski and Mésot were both seasoned international competitors and their expertise provided Barbara Ann a strong foundation in the basics of skating.

Even though her coaches recognized her potential as a skater, Barbara Ann's strict upbringing and Mary's discouraging words led to feelings of inferiority. Barbara Ann remembered, "She told me when I was a girl that I was homely, but if I was very good at what I did, I would be a success. So I always felt a little inferior, and that I had to work a little harder." She often felt she could not be as "good or polite as the next person" and constantly strove to please people. As a girl, she was also very shy. "I would sit in a corner and listen to older people talk and not participate too much," she recalled. "In fact, I was terrified of people my own age."

Barbara Ann insisted her mother always be there when she skated, so she could see a familiar face. Mary was ever-present rink side, with a pair of number nine knitting needles in her hand, making practice dresses, mitts and Angora bonnets. Barbara Ann recalled, "I was timid as a child and wanted to know she was there. Some mothers drive children and don't let them stand still a moment, but my mother used to say, 'You have done enough. We'll get some sunshine and go swimming.'"

Mary had a firm rule for Barbara Ann - music lessons were always to be the most important thing in her life, followed by school, then skating. She recalled, "We encouraged her ambition, but I told her that if she ever displayed signs of temperament, her skating was finished."

When Barbara Ann was eight, she passed her Fourth Test, won the Minto Skating Club's Devonshire Cup for Girls Under 12 and was sent down to Lake Placid to train with Walter Arian in the summer. In that year's

Minto Follies, she was "Miss 1937" in a New Year's Eve-themed number, representing "the spirit of childhood pushing away Old Father Time". The papers called her "the darling of the evening" and raved that her "grace... rivalled that of the most distinguished artists of the entire evening." Barbara Ann remembered, "I was in a tiny little white tutu dress representing the year 1936. It paid to be tiny, which is why I got the part." At this show, she was also chosen to present a bouquet to Olympic Silver Medallist Cecilia Colledge, the visiting guest star from England.

In 1938, Barbara Ann was invited to take part in the Toronto Skating Club's annual carnival and perform during the intermission of the Ottawa Public Schools Hockey Championship. She earned the Figure Skating Department of the Amateur Skating Association of Canada's Silver Medal that year as well. As a reward for passing the test, her father gave her a gold ring set, with three pearls, that he said once belonged to Queen Anne. The ring became one of Barbara Ann's most prized possessions. She also had a lucky stuffed Koala named Junior that she took with her to competitions and a musical stuffed toy horse named Susy that was her good luck charm. As she got a little older, she started bringing her Charlie McCarthy doll everywhere and came out of her shell by doing a ventriloquist act for fellow skaters and her music teacher, Miss Barnes.

Gladys Barnes taught Barbara Ann music for ten years and believed that Barbara Ann's talent in tickling the ivory keys rivalled her ability on the ice. She once remarked, 'She was always ambitious and conscientious. She had great powers of concentration and I think she would have been a success at anything she tried."

Barbara Ann played Chopin and Debussy very well but recalled how her teacher had once scolded her by saying, "When will you ever learn that skating will get you nowhere?" As skating became more important, Barbara Ann went from practising the piano two hours a day to one.

Barbara Ann's academic life also changed when she was nine. She was pulled out of the Ottawa Normal Model School and began studying with a private school tutor named Sylvia Seeley, who lived on Somerset Street West. Sylvia was also a member of the Minto Skating Club. She had taught at Ashbury College for a year and tutored several local skaters, ballet dancers and piano students.

Sylvia Seeley was Barbara Ann's tutor for ten years. Under her guidance, Barbara Ann excelled in the French, German and Latin languages. She also enjoyed history and geography. Her least favourite subject was mathematics. Sylvia described Barbara Ann as a punctual, unspoiled child with excellent concentration skills. She remarked, "I have never known B.A. to fail at anything she set her mind to... [She] was always very modest and entirely free from personal conceit. I used to say she was the happiest child I have ever known... Another thing I admired was that she was so steady, so regular - always the same - not moody one day and bright the next. She was always the same sweet girl."

A third - and very important teacher - also appeared in Barbara Ann's life in 1938: a new coach named Otto Gold. Mentored by three-time Olympic Gold Medallist Gillis Grafström, Gold took up skating in Czechoslovakia in 1916, during The Great War. He won the silver medal at the 1930 European Championships in Berlin and taught skating in Prague for several years before relocating to England, where he taught in London and skated professionally in ice pantomimes in Bournemouth. He escaped Czechoslovakia by train mere hours before the Nazis took over and escaped to Canada via England – a very fortuitous move indeed, as he was of Jewish heritage.

A strict taskmaster, Otto Gold planned every minute of Barbara Ann's days. Rising at six o'clock, she would walk across the Laurier Bridge every morning in the freezing cold. From eight until eleven, she practised the seventy-two different school figures skaters could be called on to perform in competition on patch sessions. From eleven to twelve, she practised her free skating program. During the senior practice from twelve to one, the Minto Skating Club's staff served the intermediate skaters lunch. She was back on the ice from one to four, then went home and studied with Sylvia Seeley. She often had supper in bed, while she worked on her lessons. By Mr. Gold's orders, it was lights out at 9:00. She repeated this schedule six days a week, with Sundays off for church and piano practice. In the summers in Schumacher, Kitchener or Lake Placid, practice time was cut down to five hours.

After conferring with Mr. Gold, Mary decided that Barbara Ann's skating was becoming serious enough that she needed to have a better pair of skates for free skating. Gustave Stanzione, based in New York City, had the reputation of being the best bootmaker in the business. Mr. Stanzione made Barbara Ann a beautiful pair of the high boots which were the fashion of the time, with baby buck fur and white laces that tucked into the top. The skates came at the hefty price of one hundred dollars – approximately eighteen hundred dollars in today's money. She also started wearing Strauss blades, and skated on the same ones for years, with a wedge of leather under the heel. People didn't get new skates all of the time back then, and Barbara Ann had her skates sharpened so many times that they were quite thin at the end. During her entire amateur career, her skates were sharpened by a Great War veteran named George Smith, who had emigrated from England in 1920. Smith had been sharpening the skates of Ottawa's top skaters for decades. He had a room in the store of C.H. Howe and Company on Bank Street and once sharpened Sonja Henie's skates when she came to the Minto Club to perform. Barbara Ann's skates were sharpened five or six times a season. For figures, she wore an old pair of Wilson skates that Mr. Gold brought back from England.

In December of 1938, Clyde took Barbara Ann, Mary and Mr. Gold to see Sonja Henie's Hollywood Ice Revue at the Montreal Forum. Barbara Ann had seen one of

Sonja Henie's movies and was spellbound by the Norwegian star's stage presence and costumes, but seeing her in person was a different story. She idolized Sonja from the first minute she saw her perform. During the intermission, Mr. Gold sent a note to Sonja's dressing room letting her know he was there. Mr. Gold had given Sonja lessons when she was in Prague in 1934 and skated in shows in England with Andrée and Pierre Brunet, who had won the pairs title at the 1932 Winter Olympics in Lake Placid when Sonja won her second Olympic gold medal in the ladies event. Sonja became excited and invited him backstage after the show for tea. Mr. Gold took Barbara Ann with him to her dressing room. While they chatted in a different language, Barbara Ann was completely starstruck and barely knew what to say when Sonja gave her an autographed picture.

Under Mr. Gold's tutelage, Barbara Ann became the youngest member of the Minto Skating Club to pass the Canadian First-Class test, when she was only ten years old, in 1939. That year, she also competed in the Canadian Figure Skating Championships for the first time, finishing fifth in the junior ladies event, well behind winner Therese McCarthy of Toronto. Mr. Gold recalled, "The first school figures in that competition skated by B.A. were very good and I felt she would be able to keep up that pace - but then it happened. The late [John Zalvidar] Machado, a Toronto judge in the competition - acknowledged his liking of her skating with an appreciative smile, which with B.A.'s keen observation, she could not miss. After that school figure, which was skated below her average, B.A. rushed to me and tears came rolling out of her beautiful eyes. As she calmed down, I found out that that upsetting feeling was caused by that appreciative smile of Mr. Machado. In her mind, which was set on lay-outs, tracings and re-tracings, there was no room for any smiles - that smile as she figured was a belittling smile and before we knew, the competition was over and we lost valuable points."

Another Toronto judge, John S. MacLean, made a more positive impact on Barbara Ann. He was so dazzled by her skating that he wrote her an encouraging letter that included a quote from John Milton's *Lycidas*: "Scorn delights and live laborious days." This quote made a great impression on Barbara Ann and served as a mantra when she turned down invitation after invitation to parties and theatres during her skating career.

Barbara Ann was delighted to receive invitations to skate in carnivals in Boston and New York City. Performing solos in the Skating Club of Lake Placid's winter carnival, Toronto Skating Club's carnival and the Minto Follies, she shared the ice with great champions like Megan Taylor and Montgomery 'Bud' Wilson. She didn't only rub shoulders with skating royalty that year. The Minto Follies was dubbed the Royal Minto Follies, as King George VI and Queen Elizabeth gave their Royal Patronage to the production during their Royal Tour of Canada. The patriotic spectacle was a first at the Minto Skating Club. A large British coat of arms was painted under the ice. Red and blue bunting festooned the boards. When their Majesties arrived, the audience sang "God Save The King" to the first reigning Monarchs to visit Canada. Barbara Ann skated to Strauss' "Tales from the Vienna Woods" during the Powder Puff Ballet number.

Under Mr. Gold's strict eye, Barbara Ann was starting to make a name for herself, but it wasn't all sunshine and rainbows. Though she considered Mr. Gold a "second father", in the seven years she worked with him, he only complimented her once. After she passed her Gold Medal test, he said, "Now, we'll go back to the beginning and really learn how to skate." Gold's forte was school figures, not free skating, and as hard as she worked to perfect her brackets, counters and loops, she sometimes struggled. "I'd think I had done a figure perfectly and go back and look at my track on the ice. There would be those awful flats... He [once] made me write several hundred times, 'I will bend my knee.' I scrawled it in pencil as fast as I could, and he made me do it over in ink, neatly and carefully. He felt a skater could never have enough grounding - there was always more to learn to improve."

In the summer of 1939, Barbara Ann won the senior ladies title at the first Annual Open Summer Competition in Lake Placid, defeating skaters from New York and Boston. She also won the junior pairs title, skating with Pierre Benoit of the Quebec Winter Club. These small victories did much to boost her confidence and show her that the hard work she was putting into her figures was starting to pay off.

Figure skating was the center of Barbara Ann's universe,

but her reality shifted dramatically when she and her mother arrived in Ottawa from Lake Placid on September 11, 1939. Just one day earlier, Parliament had debated and approved Great Britain's Declaration of War. Canada was officially at war.

As the daughter of the Military Secretary for the Department of National Defence, Barbara Ann understood the implications more than many other girls her age.

2

"Practice to stand up well on your skates and develop good strong ankles and edges. Never get weary of practising inside and outside edges, forwards and backwards. Practice figure eights too." - Barbara Ann Scott

World War II impacted Canadian figure skating significantly. Though most skating clubs across the country remained open, many competitors, coaches and judges joined the Army, Navy and Air Force. Others turned to war work at factories and farms. They nursed, volunteered with Red Cross blood drives and organized charity fundraisers.

The club tea room at the Minto Skating Club became known as "the knitting circle" when a group of skating mothers devoted their tea time to knitting socks, scarves and sweaters to send overseas to the front lines. The Minto Skating Club's members organized teas, bazaars and garden parties for war charities and raised money for the Red Cross at their Minto Follies.

Aimée (Haycock) Davies was one of the first Canadian Champions during the Edwardian Era and a lifelong member of the Minto Skating Club. Mrs. Davies served on the executive board of the Ottawa branch of the Canadian Red Cross Corps and was more than happy to accept help from the Scotts. Barbara Ann wore a white armband and volunteered with the Red Cross drive for funds.

Mary drove transports for the Red Cross Mobile Blood Clinic in Perth. She had the opportunity to go overseas to serve with the Red Cross but Clyde told her, "Your job is here, looking after [your] child. So I stayed."

The Scott family's maid Wilhemina wanted to go into defense work. Mary and Clyde decided it made sense to downsize and the family moved to a third-floor apartment at 162 Metcalfe Street.

In 1940, Barbara Ann won the junior ladies title on home ice at the Canadian Figure Skating Championships in Ottawa. The youngest of the eight skaters competing, she showed grace and maturity beyond her years in a free skating performance set to selections from Gonoud's "Faust". By this time, she had already mastered the double Salchow and double loop jumps.

After the event, Kaye D. Carlcton asked eleven-year-old Barbara Ann if she wanted to make a career of skating. She responded, "Oh gracious no. I just skate because I love it. I do lots of other things: I play the piano, swim, golf with my Mummy and Daddy, climb trees and play with my dolls. I just love to read and I like to study French and German, too. My two greatest desires are to ride a horse, which my instructors won't permit, and to be a flower girl at a wedding."

In May, the Associated Screen News released a Canadian Cameo newsreel directed by Gordon Stirling called

Flashing Blades, featuring Barbara Ann, World Champion Megan Taylor and Canadian Champion Montgomery 'Bud' Wilson. The short film played before moving pictures at theatres in Montreal and Ottawa. It was the first of many such newsreels that acquainted the general public with Barbara Ann's skating.

In January of 1941, Otto Gold married his British fiancée Eva Steven in a small ceremony in the Scott family's apartment. The couple hadn't seen each other in fifteen months, but Eva was able to secure passage to Canada after being hired as a coach at the Kitchener-Waterloo Skating Club. Clyde gave away the bride and twelve-year-old Barbara Ann got to fulfill her wish of being a flower girl. Later that month, Barbara Ann competed in the senior women's event at the Canadian Figure Skating Championships for the first time, at The Winter Club in Montreal. She finished a surprising second behind nineteen-year-old Mary Rose Thacker of Winnipeg. Mary Rose had gone overseas to train with Mr. Gold when he was coaching in England and come to Ontario to train with him sporadically. Mr. Gold gave both Mary Rose and Barbara Ann the same music for their free skating program that year – the "Modřanská" (Beer Barrel) Polka. Barbara Ann was quite surprised to have placed so high in her senior debut at Canadians, as nearly all of the competitors had performed particularly well.

Barbara Ann's success at the Canadian Figure Skating Championships led to an invitation to represent Canada at the North American Figure Skating Championships in

Ardmore, Pennsylvania ten days later. It was an inauspicious international debut. Mary took Barbara Ann to an American doctor not long after they arrived, as she was suffering from a fever and chills. An hour before the competition, she was diagnosed with the German measles. She placed a disappointing sixth overall, over one hundred points behind Mary Rose Thacker. After the competition, she was quarantined at the hotel with Mary. She couldn't grasp why she was confined to a gloomy room for days on end, with no radio to lift her spirits. The family had their own car, and there was no risk of spreading anything if they simply drove home without stopping. When she was finally permitted to leave, she quietly slipped out to the car, her face hidden by a shawl.

In July, Clyde made a dangerous wartime trip to England with Hon. Ian MacKenzie, the Canadian Minister of Pensions and Welfare. The experiences of Londoners on the home front were a world apart from what Canadians were experiencing. Blackout curtains, air raid sirens, rationing books, Anderson shelters and gas masks were daily realities during The Blitz – realities that Canadians hoped to never experience. The purpose of the trip was a series of strategic meetings with British military and government officials. Clyde had the honour of visiting 10 Downing Street and personally presenting British Prime Minister Winston Churchill with Canada's Victory Torch and money raised through a connected campaign. While in England, he visited former Canadian Prime Minister Viscount Bennett, Barbara Ann's godfather. On September 4, 1941, Clyde was invited to a dinner at the home of Arza Clair Casselman, the Conservative Member of Parliament for Grenville-Dundas. He had gone specifically to see Grote Stirling, a former Minister of National Defense, who was a guest at the Casselman home. As he was saying his goodbyes at 1:30 in the morning, a large piece of shrapnel that had not been removed in his many surgeries shifted and hit his heart. He suffered a fatal heart attack and dropped dead at the Casselmans door. Clyde's death came as a massive shock to Barbara Ann and Mary, who had been away since June and were on their way back from Kitchener at the time the news broke. Throughout his life, Clyde had never talked about his military service or his near-death experience in Belgium during The Great War. He devoted himself wholly to his work and always looked forward, never back. Barbara Ann recalled, "I used to practice eight hours a day and think I was working very hard, and then I would come home and find him still working, sometimes long after midnight. No matter how tired he was, he never stopped."

After Clyde's death, money became a very real problem for Mary. She economized in every way possible to pay for Barbara Ann's skating and travel expenses. It all had to come out of a pension of about three thousand dollars a year, and in those days, skaters didn't receive any significant financial support from the Canadian Figure Skating Association because they simply didn't have the money. Skaters were on their own and under the strict rules governing amateurism at the time, they weren't allowed to significantly profit from their skating. Barbara Ann and Mary simply had to make do somehow, one way or another.

3

"Remember that the more technical fine points are not what they come to see. They want to be amused or startled." - *Barbara Ann Scott*

Though times were tough, Barbara Ann 'kept calm and carried on.' After months of training, she and fellow Minto Skating Club member Gwenneth Steeves became the first Canadians to pass the revised Gold (8th) Test of the United States Figure Skating Association. Only one other skater, Phebe Tucker, had passed all the Canadian and U.S. tests.

At the 1942 Canadian Figure Skating Championships in Winnipeg, Barbara Ann again finished second behind Mary Rose Thacker, the hometown favourite. At this event, she made history as the first woman to start her program with a double Lutz at the Canadian Championships. Some felt she didn't receive the marks she deserved. Alison Chown remarked, "Her free skating exhibition... left the crowd breathless. Her program was packed with difficult jumps and spins and together with her radiating personality and the ease with which she did her jumps, made her performance a delight to watch." That fall, the Winnipeg Winter Club was converted into a naval training center.

Barbara Ann was invited to guest star in the Halifax Skating Assembly's carnival Carry On. The production raised nearly a thousand dollars for the Queen's Canadian Fund. At the Minto Follies in Ottawa, Barbara Ann headlined with Freddie Tomlins.

Freddie was an affable and incredibly talented young British skater who had competed in the 1936 Winter Olympics in Garmisch-Partenkirchen. He was famously thrown out of the rink, skates and all, by the S.S. Guards after barging through a crowd, handing Hitler himself a pencil and asking for his autograph. At the last World Figure Skating Championships before the war, he and Graham Sharp went out for several pints of lager right before the men's free skate, where they won the gold and silver medals. Freddie later earned his Pilot's Officer certificate at the Royal Canadian Air Force base in Trenton and was stationed at a Coastal Command station in Cornwall, England. In 1943, he was tragically killed while serving as an air gunner during an operational flight over the English Channel, his plane presumably shot down by a Nazi submarine.

The news of Freddie's tragic death filled Mary with a sense of dread. Her only son, William, was serving as a bomber pilot in the Royal Canadian Air Force. She no doubt anxiously waited for letters from him and in private moments, looked at his photograph and prayed.

Luckily, William survived the War. He later worked as a Chief Pilot with World Wide Aviation Agencies, delivering aircraft to buyers in Europe, The Caribbean and South America. He eventually settled in British Honduras (now Belize) with his wife and children.

Due to wartime conditions and the considerable number of skaters either serving or engaged in war work, the 1943 Canadian Figure Skating Championships in Toronto were cancelled. Barbara Ann continued to hone her skills by appearing in carnivals in Halifax and Kingston, performing as a pair with Sergeant Donald Gilchrist, who was serving with the Royal Canadian Army Service Corps. By then, she was also working at a canteen in Ottawa three days a week. It served hundreds of lunches to those in service.

The Canadian Figure Skating Championships returned in 1944, but the senior men's, pairs, ice dance and fours events were all cancelled because so many men had enlisted. Mary Rose Thacker had retired from competitive skating after the 1942 Canadian Championships, married a Winnipeg Grenadier in Flin Flon and moved to Jamaica. Mary Rose's retirement made Barbara Ann the new favourite to win the Canadian title. With a lead of one hundred and fifty-seven points after the compulsory figures, she trounced her competitors and was the unanimous winner. The 1944 Winter Olympic Games, slated to be held in Cortina d'Ampezzo, had long before been called off. The European and World Figure Skating Championships were also postponed during the War, so the new Canadian Champion didn't yet have a chance to test her mettle against the best skaters of Europe. That's not to say she didn't have friendly rivals.

While Barbara Ann was earning accolades in Canada, another teenager, Gretchen Van Zandt Merrill, was winning every event she entered in the United States. Gretchen grew up in the affluent Boston suburb of Chestnut Hill and had quite a bit in common with Barbara Ann. They both lost their fathers at young ages, met Sonja Henie and were privately tutored. Their skating styles were quite different though. Barbara Ann's strength was her consistency in school figures, whereas Gretchen struggled in the figures but excelled in free skating. Barbara Ann's image was more "girl-next-door"; Gretchen's was more "glamour girl". Gretchen's late grandfather, an old money millionaire, left her a fortune. It bought her expensive dresses that the Scotts, on a government pension, couldn't afford. Gretchen was coached by former Olympic Medallist Maribel Vinson Owen for much of her career. She also worked with Mr. Gold when she attended his summer school in Kitchener. As had been the case when Mr. Gold worked with Mary Rose Thacker, sharing a coach with her competitor had only encouraged Barbara Ann to succeed even more.

After repeating as Canadian Champion in 1945, sixteen-year-old Barbara Ann travelled to New York City to compete at the North American Figure Skating Championships at Madison Square Garden. When she competed in this event in 1941, she had been quite sick and finished well below Gretchen. This time around, the tables turned. With a dazzling performance, she defeated Gretchen four judges to two, making history as the youngest champion ever at the North American Championships. Many years later, Barbara Ann still felt her performance at this event was her best ever in competition.

After winning the North American title, Barbara Ann went on a whirlwind tour, flying from New York to Vancouver to skate in the Connaught Skating Club's carnival, then to Ottawa for the Minto Follies and back down to the United States for carnivals in Baltimore and New York City.

On September 2, 1945, the Japanese formally surrendered in Tokyo Bay, officially ending World War II. As one chapter in history ended, another one played out on the ice.

4

"I'm a Canadian, and tremendously proud to be one. I don't think we're such a bad lot." - Barbara Ann Scott

The end of the war didn't mean an immediate return to business as usual in the figure skating world. Barbara Ann defended her national title with ease at the 1946 Canadian Figure Skating Championships in Schumacher, Ontario. Unfortunately the International Skating Union was still in a rebuilding process and was not yet ready to restart the European and World Figure Skating Championships. Her season ended with a series of Canadian carnivals rather than a trip overseas to compete for international honours.

When Barbara Ann travelled to North Bay, she was met at the train station by a member of the Wiikwemkoong First Nation and pulled into town on a sleigh by five Seppala Siberian Sleddogs. The North Bay carnival had a Northern theme of "a Hudson Bay trading post flanked by trees and Totem poles." The special guests for the show were the famous Dionne Quintuplets, who were born in nearby Corbeil.

In the summer, Barbara Ann found time for a new hobby – flying. She took lessons at the Ottawa Flying Club and quickly earned her student's pilot license. She made history as the youngest woman from the Club to fly solo. She told one reporter, "I have only a student license now and can only fly around the field with a big sign on my plane that says 'Beware, Student.'" She eventually earned her private license. But, during the test, she opened the plane's door and leaned out to get a better look while landing and got a face full of mud.

In the fall of 1946, Barbara Ann received some unexpected and life-changing news. Mr. Gold, her longtime coach, had accepted a new position as head professional at the Vancouver Skating Club. The rumour among the staff at the Minto Skating Club was that Melville Rogers fired him.

Following Mr. Gold out west was not an option. The family's life was in Ottawa and the Minto Skating Club was Barbara Ann's second home. "Otto Gold left me flat in 1946," she recalled. "It broke my heart. I was in tears. I went to Eva Gold, and she said, 'There's nothing I can do.'"

It took the Minto Skating Club several months to find a new professional to replace Mr. Gold. In the interim, Melville Rogers and Donald B. Cruikshank came to the rink every morning before they went to the office to help coach Barbara Ann. Though the assistance of two former Canadian Champions was very much appreciated, Melville and Donald were not coaches – and they had full-time day jobs. They were relieved when the Minto Skating Club hired Sheldon Galbraith in November. The handsome young coach began teaching at the club in December after his discharge from the United States Naval Air Corps came through. Veteran sportswriter Jim Proudfoot remembered, "Galbraith was shrewd and stern in an era when skating was still something of a genteel social affair, like polo or the waltz. To his athletes, he was Mr. Galbraith, never Sheldon. They were in awe of him. And that was the proper attitude; his smarts usually gave them an edge."

Mr. Galbraith had first seen Barbara Ann skate at the 1941 Canadian Figure Skating Championships in Montreal when he was in town performing with the Ice Follies. Barbara Ann remembered, "The first time [he] ever saw me he said, 'You look like a milk bottle - small on top and too big in the legs.' I think that's why I've apologized for myself all my life."

Despite the rocky introduction, Barbara Ann and Mr. Galbraith clicked immediately and she found adapting to his style of coaching easy. "Right from the beginning, Barbara Ann and I were a team," Mr. Galbraith recalled. "She was always eager to learn and I was delighted to have so earnest a pupil. I didn't have to teach her diligence or perseverance. She was born with that." Barbara Ann remembered her coach as "an entirely agreeable man [who] never missed any tricks, either."

Based on her result at the 1946 Canadian Figure Skating Championships, Barbara Ann was selected to travel overseas to represent Canada at the European and World Figure Skating Championships. There were three problems, though.

Firstly, Barbara Ann only had a matter of weeks to

practice her free skating program to "Only Make Believe" from the musical *Showboat*. Mr. Galbraith had come up with the sentimental new program because he didn't think that the music Mr. Gold had chosen for Barbara Ann did her justice.

The second problem was that Mary simply did not have the means to cover the travel costs of sending Barbara Ann, Mr. Galbraith, and herself to Europe for an extended period of time. Donald B. Cruikshank and Melville Rogers intervened by sending a letter to Mayor Stanley Lewis, suggesting that a fund be set up to cover Barbara Ann's travel expenses. This campaign raised approximately ten thousand dollars in ten days, from less than two dozen prominent Ottawa businessmen. The Canadian Figure Skating Association chipped in fifteen hundred dollars.

The third issue was the matter of Mr. Galbraith's leave of absence from the Minto Skating Club. The club was in a tricky spot, because the other skaters also required his attention, but they recognized the need to send him and ultimately agreed to it.

Barbara Ann, Mary, Mr. Galbraith and family friend, Betty Caldwell flew from Montreal to Prestwick, Scotland in January of 1947. They spent four days in London before flying to Switzerland and taking a train to Davos. They arrived several weeks before the European Figure Skating Championships were set to begin. International figure skating competitions in Europe at the time were largely held on outdoor rinks, and Europeans called North Americans "hothouse skaters", because they tended to struggle with acclimatizing themselves to the harsh conditions of skating outdoors – wind, snow, rain, slush, poor ice and cold temperatures. Barbara Ann was no stranger to the cold, as the temperatures in the Minto Skating Club's Waller Street rink would sometimes reach twenty below. Sometimes her feet would be so cold that she'd put them on the radiators in the dressing room to warm up, even though she was warned she would get chilblains. However, dealing with the wind and snow were challenges she rarely faced in Canada – though Government House in Ottawa had allowed her to practice on its outdoor rink briefly before she left for Europe.

At first, Barbara Ann found the wind quite challenging, particularly when practicing compulsory figures, but with Mr. Galbraith's help and hours upon hours of practice, she learned to adapt. "No hour was too early or too late; no temperature too low or wind too raw. On brittle ice or slushy surface, Barbara Ann was on hand to put in the necessary practice," remembered Mr. Galbraith. "Barbara Ann skated after dark when it was colder, with only the aid of snowballs, which were placed at strategic points about her school figures when there was no electric lighting for night practice. Never once did she waver or complain... The most important thing to remember is that Barbara capitalized on every asset and advantage. She left nothing to chance. In her case no effort was too great and no sacrifice too much if it benefited her skating. That came first."

Barbara Ann wasn't the only one to arrive in Davos early to acclimatize to the weather conditions. Gretchen Van Zandt Merrill was in town as well, working with famed Swiss coach Arnold Gerschwiler. She garnered considerable media attention by entering and winning a minor international competition soon after she arrived. The press harassed Gretchen so much that during the competition, she almost kicked a photographer. He was lying down on the ice, just inches away, while she was doing one of her figures. British judge T.D. Richardson remembered that Gretchen was "very funny when she came off the ice. With a mixture of anger and amusement, she said: 'What is this anyway? Hollywood?'"

Barbara Ann had a forty-one-point lead over British skater Daphne Walker and Gretchen Van Zandt Merrill after the compulsory figures at the 1947 European Figure Skating Championships. Though her rivals from Britain and the United States both performed exceptionally well in the free skate, Barbara Ann gave an outstanding performance of her own to win the competition five judges to two. It was the first time in history a Canadian skater won a gold medal at the European Championships.

After her performance ended, Barbara Ann looked up and saw that nearly everyone in Davos had come to see her skate. The locals even gave her a nickname – Barbarelli. "Davos was so good to me," recalled Barbara Ann. "They kind of adopted me, which was so nice... I thought Daddy would be pleased."

From Davos, Barbara Ann and her entourage travelled to St. Moritz, then north to Stockholm, Sweden for the World Figure Skating Championships. Conditions in Stockholm were worse than in Davos. The enormous outdoor rink where the competition was held was partially sheltered by buildings on three sides, but the wind and snow swept through and temperatures dipped to twenty below. Barbara Ann said that the "ice was as hard as a cement floor" and she wished she could have competed in her fur coat. For warmth, she wore a white galyak dress, which from a distance looked like silk brocade. She was one of the only skaters to be savvy enough to wear sunglasses when doing compulsory figures, to offset the sun's glare.

As in Davos, Barbara Ann amassed a considerable lead in the figures and earned two perfect 6.0's in the free skate. She made history as the first Canadian skater – man or woman – to win a gold medal at the World Championships. British skater Daphne Walker finished second and American skater Gretchen Van Zandt Merrill was third. Notably missing from the cheering audience the evening of the free skate was King Gustaf V, who was unable to attend because he was in mourning. His grandson, an heir apparent to the Swedish throne, had just perished in the same plane crash that killed American actress and singer Grace Moore.

Though Mr. Galbraith described the Swedish people as "most cordial", Barbara Ann was unsettled by an experience that took place after a post-competition exhibition. "The crowds - made up of people eight feet tall, I'll swear - swarmed on the ice, crowded around me and just stared," she recalled. "They didn't say anything I could understand, and they didn't do anything but push and shove. It took 40 minutes for me to get off the rink, and by that time I was getting pretty panicky." Barbara Ann escaped from the crowd by entering a random door and walking down a long tunnel to a caretaker's home, where a family was sitting at a table having supper.

Barbara Ann's victory in Stockholm earned high praise from Ulrich Salchow, the International Skating Union's President and the first man to win an Olympic gold medal, back in 1908 when figure skating was a Summer Olympic sport. It also came as a great relief to the Director of the Canadian Travel Bureau. D. Leo Dolan was so confident in Barbara Ann's victory in Stockholm that he took a gamble and included a photo of her with the caption "Women's Figure Skating Champion of the World" in the Bureau's annual brochure. Two hundred thousand copies were printed in December of 1946 before she had even left for Europe. Dolan remarked, "Had Barbara Ann not won... I would have been a marked man."

As news of Barbara Ann's victory spread to Ottawa, Prime Minister William Lyon Mackenzie King sent a cable to Stockholm congratulating his talented constituent Barbara Ann on her win. In his diary, he wrote, "I have derived a tremendous pleasure out of that young girl's success. It is really a national event of very great significance."

Another event of significance at the time was the birth of Donald B. Cruikshank's daughter – on Valentine's Day, 1947, while he was in Stockholm serving as the Canadian judge on the panel that awarded Barbara Ann the gold medal at the World Championships. Donald's daughter was named Barbara Ann – and Barbara Ann Scott became her godmother.

After her victory in Stockholm, Barbara Ann went on a week-long tour of Europe, giving performances in Paris, Prague and London. In Prague, it snowed so hard that they had to clear the ice every fifteen minutes. Fittingly, the new "Queen of the Ice" crossed the Atlantic in style on the Cunard White Star Line's Queen Elizabeth, arriving in New York City and travelling north to Canada by train.

Before Barbara Ann arrived in Canada, Mother Marie Thomas D'Aquin, a nun from France who started the Sisters of the Jeanne d'Arc Institute in Ottawa, published a lovely poem in her honour.

The grand welcome Barbara Ann received upon her return was truly historic.

5

"She put figure skating on the map. She made it a major sport in Canada." - Larry O'Brien

Barbara Ann's train chug-a-lugged into the Montreal West Station at just after eight o'clock in the morning on March 7, 1947. Reporters and curious early morning commuters seeking autographs elbowed each other to get closer as she stepped out onto the platform sporting a new straw bonnet gifted to her by the Canadian Consul General in New York. "I'm happy to be home again," she said to a Montreal journalist. "All I missed was Canada."

Barbara Ann's homecoming in Ottawa was a huge deal. Seventy thousand people lined the streets awaiting the arrival of her train and children were given an extended lunch break at school to attend her homecoming. The Superfluity Shop on Nicholas Street designed a window display featuring a toy skating figure delicately hung by a wire over a sparkling glass rink. The wire was rigged so that the miniature version of Barbara Ann looked like it was moving across the ice. Two local men, George Cullen and Ted Gray, collaborated to write an original song - a waltz called "Barbara Ann Scott is Skating". It was played at the Chateau Laurier and on CBO radio. The lyrics of the song were as follows:

Barbara Ann Scott is Skating

So gaily on her way
Barbara Ann is skating
With a sunny smile so gay,

Perfection is her duty,
And from the very start
So charming is her beauty
She captures ev'ry heart.

Music is softly playing
A dreamy melody
Canada's Pride is skating,
Gliding gracefully.

Barbara Ann is Skating
And always smiling through;
A vision captivating -
We are all so proud of you.

When Barbara Ann got off the train at Union Station at just after half past eleven, she was greeted by Mayor Stanley Lewis, members of the Board of Control and the band of the Governor General's Foot Guards, who played "Let Me Call You Sweetheart". The Mayor then escorted her to a canary yellow Buick Phaeton convertible with leather upholstery and push-button windows, bearing the license plate "47-U1". The City paid thirty-five hundred dollars for the car and the clever license plate was the brainchild of J. Grant Shaw, a member of the City Council who also happened to be the issuer of automobile licenses for the city. Barbara Ann's car led a ticker-tape parade through the snowy streets of Ottawa, with her in the lead car and Mary, Mr. Galbraith and Donald B. Cruikshank in the second. At a civic reception that followed at the Chateau Laurier, the Mayor gave her the keys to "47-U1". Barbara Ann recalled, "I couldn't believe it. I thought maybe a few friends would come and greet me at the station... I couldn't believe that anybody would care that much."

It was the largest gathering in Canada's capital since the royal visit of King George VI and Queen Elizabeth in 1939, and the scene was quite rowdy. Mayor Lewis asserted, "The crowds were harder to handle than during the visit of the King and Queen. On that occasion, they were more restrained. It was a kid's day, and they made the most of it. I was afraid we were going to run over some of them. They wouldn't move out of the way for police, motorcycles or the automobiles. Some even tried to climb up on the car."

The Prime Minister was unable to attend Barbara Ann's homecoming as he was suffering from the flu, but he sent Hon. Ian Mackenzie to represent him at the festivities, with a handwritten letter addressed to Barbara Ann. He wrote in his diary, "I am really sorry to miss this event, for I have felt a keen interest in the triumph of that little girl." Hon. MacKenzie presented a motion extending "warmest greetings and good wishes" to Barbara Ann in the House of Commons. This resolution, presented by the Liberal Party, was seconded by Hon. John Bracken, the leader of the Conservative Party.

Barbara Ann was the first figure skater to be honoured in Canada's Parliament. The fact that she deserved such a tribute was one of the very few things that both parties could agree on. An identical scenario played out in the Legislative Assembly of Ottawa, where leaders of the Conservative, Liberal and Canadian Cooperative Federation parties unanimously agreed to honour Barbara Ann. Gladys Strum, the fifth woman in history to be elected to the House of Commons, said that "women of Canada were coming into their own". She hoped Barbara Ann's achievements would usher in "a day when half the benches will be occupied by the Barbara Ann Scotts of this country."

After her Ottawa homecoming, Barbara Ann, Mary and Betty drove "47-U1" to Betty's parents' home in Prescott. Barbara Ann remembered, "We had the windows down, and when it started to snow we couldn't get them up! They were stuck in that brand new car." The new-fangled push-button windows would be the least of Barbara Ann's worries when it came to the new car.

The strict rules governing amateurism of the time dictated that skaters could not accept gifts valued at more than twenty-five dollars. People were already squawking about the car the day she received it. Sydney Dawes, the President of the Canadian Olympic Committee, told the press that as far as they and the Amateur Athletic Union of Canada were concerned, all that was necessary was for them to approve the gifts before they were accepted. Barbara Ann had been assured by Mayor Stanley Lewis and the other adults in the room that all of the formalities had been taken care of, and that she had nothing to be worried about.

In the weeks that followed, Barbara Ann travelled to Montreal and Toronto for ticker-tape parades and receptions. Both parades drew thousands more well-wishers. In Toronto, police shooed VIPs out of the way to allow children who had been waiting hours to see Barbara Ann a chance to move closer for a better view. The city suspended its anti-noise by-law for twenty minutes so people could make all of the noise they wanted. People threw confetti from office windows on Bay Street. Eaton's took out a full-page advertisement in the newspaper welcoming Barbara Ann to the city. She also found time to skate in the Rotary Club Carnival at Maple Leaf Gardens in Toronto, which raised thousands of dollars for victims of the Thames flood in England.

These parades, receptions and carnivals, along with dozens more, ate into Barbara Ann's training time, but you wouldn't have known it if you watched her skate at the 1947 North American Figure Skating Championships, held at the Minto Skating Club. Barbara Ann unanimously defended her North American title, defeating Janette Ahrens, Yvonne Sherman and fellow Ontarian Suzanne Morrow. Gretchen Van Zandt Merrill was a no-show. Canadian journalists, hungry for 'a scoop', insinuated that "the American champion did not care to face the Canadian titleholder." In reality, Barbara Ann and Gretchen got along just fine, and Gretchen had planned a vacation in California long before the competition.

Two months after Barbara Ann accepted "47-U1", Canadian sports journalists learned that the International Olympic Committee's President Sigfrid Edström had made an inquiry to the Canadian Olympic Association about her amateur status. The matter had been brought to Edström's attention in a private letter from Avery Brundage, the President of the United States Olympic Committee and the International Olympic Committee's Vice-President. Brundage claimed that Barbara Ann's acceptance of the car was a violation of the Olympic Code, which stated that "amateur athletes could not accept gifts, money, or advantages of a material character." Brundage opened one heck of a can of worms because it was a widely-known open secret that the father of Sonja Henie, the most recent Olympic Gold Medallist in women's figure skating, had accepted many lavish gifts – including more than one automobile – during his daughter's reign. Further to this, Barbara Ann was well-assured by officials that she was allowed to accept the car.

Not everyone was thrilled about "47-U1" being bought at the expense of the taxpayers in the first place. One disgruntled Manitoban wrote an angry letter to the editor of the *Winnipeg Tribune*. They bemoaned the fact that while Barbara Ann was receiving a brand-new car as a gift for her figure skating success, a veteran who earned the Victoria Cross was working as a janitor at the Parliament Building in Ottawa, stressing the inadequate housing, training allowances and poor pay veterans received. It was a classic case of whataboutism.

Sports historian Stephen R. Wenn asserted that Avery Brundage was the victim of a "vicious and cynical media attack" as a result of the media firestorm that took place over the car. He wasn't particularly well-liked to start with. His staunch views on amateurism were regarded as outdated and he was quite grudging about women participating in the Olympics at all. Once Brundage learned that Barbara Ann had been told by officials that her acceptance of the car wouldn't affect her amateur status, his view on the matter softened, but the damage had already been done because he had chosen to "shoot first and ask questions later."

The Canadian Olympic Association got some flack as well, as some believed they should have shown more backbone and stood up to Brundage and the International Olympic Committee. The Prime Minister even got involved, asking J.C. Patteson, Canada's representative on the International Olympic Committee, to "safeguard Scott's interest." To add fuel to the fire, Barbara Ann and Mary inferred to the press that Americans might have wished to oust her from the Olympic Games.

The Canadian press theorized it was all a conspiracy to better Gretchen Van Zandt Merrill's gold medal chances. Toronto sports journalist Alexandrine Gibb's attempt to drum up some dirt on Gretchen backfired. She had starred in a newsreel called *Skating Lady*, which was screened in American theatres alongside the RKO film

Three Little Girls in Blue. Had the journalist watched the film in question, she would have known that the newsreel was very clearly endorsed by the United States Figure Skating Association. When Avery Brundage was asked about the situation with Gretchen, he asked, "Is she another Canadian?"

After much hullabaloo, Barbara Ann returned "47-U1" to the city at the Canadian Olympic Association's suggestion, making it very clear that she had no intention of doing anything that would in any way prevent her from representing Canada at the Olympics the following year. As a city grant had been used to buy the car, by-laws stipulated that the City of Ottawa couldn't sell the car or give it away, so it sat in the showroom of the dealer it was purchased from and became a highlight of a local sightseeing tour. Later, when Barbara Ann ran into Avery Brundage in Europe, she thanked him for bringing up the issue when he did, as it gave her the time necessary to clear herself of any charges well before the Games.

Barbara Ann received thousands of fan letters, many of which criticized Avery Brundage and sympathized with the fact she had to return the car. The fan mail situation got so out of control that Mary enlisted the help of Eileen Hodgson, a former secretary of her husband's, to answer Barbara Ann's mail and send out autographed photos. Letters arrived from all over the world – even Russia, New Zealand and Venezuela. She also received many unique gifts. A little boy from Alberta sent her his most prized possession, a knife carved out of a horn. A former German POW sent her a ring given to him by a German general. An eighty-five-year-old man knitted her a pair of mittens. Pins, handicrafts, shell brooches, handkerchiefs, make-up contacts, belts, socks, Dutch bonnets, flowers and toy animals all arrived in the ever-increasing sea of fan mail.

The Canadian Figure Skating Association's President Norman V.S. Gregory received a letter of his own from Walter S. Powell, the American representative at the International Skating Union's Congress in Oslo. Powell advised Gregory that a decision had been made to no longer allow North American skaters to compete at the European Championships, but that they would be permitted to compete in 1948 as "it would be anything but sporting to introduce that limiting rule the first year that a North American skater won the European championship." Though this letter confirmed that future generations of Canadian skaters would not be allowed to compete at the European Championships, Barbara Ann would be allowed to attempt to defend her title.

In June, Barbara Ann and Mary met Prime Minister William Lyon Mackenzie King at a reception in Ottawa. In his diary, he wrote, "Had [a] pleasant... long talk with Barbara Ann Scott and her mother. Barbara looked much too thin. I told her she must take all the rest she can. There is a very terrible danger of her overtaxing her strength. It is the first time I have seen her since her return from abroad. She spoke particularly of what the telegram she had received in Europe had meant to her at that time."

In the summer of 1947, Barbara Ann trained at the Porcupine Skating Club's summer school in Schumacher alongside two other skaters who would also compete at the Olympics the following year, Jiřina Nekolová of Czechoslovakia and Yvonne Sherman of the United States. It was announced that Daphne Walker, the British runner-up at the European and World Figure Skating Championships, had turned professional. Though Barbara Ann was the favourite, there was a group of about a half-dozen skaters who were expected to seriously challenge her and Gretchen Van Zandt Merrill for the title.

Barbara Ann and Prime Minister William Lyon Mackenzie King's paths crossed again in August of 1947. In his diary, the Prime Minister wrote, "Mr. Marshall and I went to meet Barbara Ann Scott, who arrived with her mother on a sea plane, which Barbara christened. She had to try about 10 times before the bottle burst. She had with her a little girl from Czechoslovakia who had been one of her competitors. A lovely child. I drove with the two of them over to the large motor building where Barbara was to address a meeting of teenagers. I enjoyed immensely the drive with these two young people who were most attractive and so natural. The teenagers meeting was quite a sight. I said a few words to the effect they were teenagers and I was an old ager. Referred to Barbara having brought honour to her country in all the countries she had visited in Europe. We had many photographs taken together... Later we visited the French Building, on the way stopping in at an Old York pioneer building, seeing a desk which my grandfather Mackenzie used in Parliament at the time of the Rebellion."

In the fall of 1947, Jiřina Nekolová came to Ottawa to train at the Minto Skating Club with Mr. Galbraith. Though they spoke a different language, Barbara Ann and Jiřina developed a close friendship. Not long into the skating season, the Canadian Figure Skating Association made the official announcement that Barbara Ann would be representing Canada at the 1948 Winter Olympic Games in St. Moritz, Switzerland.

To cover the expenses of sending Barbara Ann, Mary and Mr. Galbraith back to Europe for the competitive season, the Minto Skating Club worked with Mayor Stanley Lewis to establish the Mayor of Ottawa Fund, which solicited donations from the general public. Melville Rogers stressed to the public that if enough money wasn't raised, Barbara Ann wouldn't be able to go to the Olympics. With significant donations from Montreal, the fund raised more than three thousand dollars above its seven thousand dollar goal.

Barbara Ann gave her final Canadian performance before heading overseas at the Ottawa Auditorium, at an Olympic Night hockey game between the R.C.A.F. Flyers and McGill Red Men. At this event, she was presented with the National Council on Physical Fitness' National Amateur Athletic Achievement Award.

On the evening of December 14, 1947, Barbara Ann, Mary, Mr. Galbraith and family friend Margaret

McGuinness boarded a Trans-Canada Airlines flight in Montreal.

They were in for an adventure of a lifetime.

6

"There was nobody to challenge her who was better in one particular area, either compulsory figures or free skating. Everything was right. Everything was perfect. She was delicate, precise, exact, meticulous." - Dick Button

Barbara Ann's flight was delayed leaving Montreal by ten hours. After crossing the Atlantic to Prestwick, Scotland, she took a second flight to London, arriving at Heathrow Airport at eleven o'clock at night on December 15, 1947.

Post-war England was a culture shock for Barbara Ann. Unemployment was at a high and morale was at a low. Rationing was still in effect, and the skaters in England didn't have much food in their bellies. "We feel so ashamed at all we get to eat in Canada when there's so little over here. I will try not to eat too much during the couple of days I am in London," she said to a British reporter.

Barbara Ann, Mary, Margaret and Mr. Galbraith left London for Davos less than two days later. Switzerland at Christmas time was almost like a snow globe come to life, but the holidays were the farthest thing from Barbara Ann's mind. Davos was over fifteen hundred meters above sea level, and St. Moritz would be even higher, so she needed to acclimatize herself to skating at such a high altitude.

Mr. Galbraith wrote to Donald B. Cruikshank about how things were going in Davos: "Rain [was] falling nearly all the time. We have here with us a 'Life' photographer who is taking a complete series of B.A.'s training and daily [routine] etc... Most of the villagers tell us this is the worst stretch of weather they can remember so we look forward to better weather for the competitions. We are told even in Prague it is raining... B.A. skated with Hans [Gerschwiler] in the afternoon and we all bet on whether we could successfully jump double loops and flips etc. on the mush. B.A. did every jump without a miss. She also took me for 7 francs as I didn't successfully do my double loop on the first attempt. All I did was dig a rut in the ice. She is 'on the bit' as they say and spirits are fine... Maribel Vinson Owen is over now, having come on the train from Geneva as far as Davos with Jimmy Grogan and Mrs. Moore. She is to be Gretchen's trainer."

After weeks of practice under less-than-ideal conditions in Davos, Barbara Ann flew to Prague, Czechoslovakia with U.S. Champion Dick Button. After their arrival at the Ruzyně airport, Barbara Ann, Mary, Margaret and Mr. Galbraith made their way in the rain to check in at the Hotel Opera. She was soon visited by Jiřina Nekolová and her Czechoslovakian coach Dr. Vladimir Koudelka. When she arrived at the rink, she found that conditions were worse than in Davos. At one practice at four o'clock in the morning, she went through her school figures in two inches of water.

The ice conditions were so poor during the compulsory

figures that at one point, the competition was briefly stopped. Barbara Ann recalled, "The water had melted the ice down and it was all bumpy, but not covered with water now - now it was slush. [The] wind was blowing, harsh and mean and strong." After the competition restarted, Barbara Ann took a narrow four-point lead over Jiřína Nekolová, Ája Zanová, Eva Pawlik and Jeannette Altwegg.

Twelve thousand spectators showed up for the free skate, some paying scalper's prices for tickets. Barbara Ann was feeling lucky in her green chiffon dress on the day of the free skate, but lady luck was almost not on her side. Mr. Galbraith recalled, "The free skating portion of the program took place during the evening, and the place was packed to capacity. She started her routine and was about one minute and fifteen seconds into it when the record-playing needle slid off the record. The phonograph records of the period were 78rpm and the needle vibrated sideways in its track to create the sound. The groove had been worn too much to hold onto its track. These records were made with a thin layer of material poured onto a round aluminum platter. They were guaranteed for six plays and then only if you used a cactus needle! Barbara Ann's solo record was turned onto its reverse side where a backup copy was located."

Barbara Ann remembered, "I got as far as the spin when all of a sudden there was a great squeak and the record stopped. I thought for a second: 'Now what shall I do? Shall I stop? Will that count against me? Shall I go on without the music?' But of course, every step of my program is set to a certain part of the music, so if I kept going and the record was put on again the chances were that I wouldn't be able to synchronize with it. I had four minutes and no more... So I skated to the starting place and waited. Fortunately, the referee agreed with me that [it] was the right thing to do. When the record went on again I started from the beginning... I was not penalized. All seven judges placed me first, with Eva Pawlik coming in second. It was said that my score was the highest ever awarded in Prague, seven placings and 181.6 points."

After it was announced that she had successfully defended her European title, the crowd went berserk, stomping, whistling and shouting "Scottová! Scottová!" Václav Vacek, the Mayor of Prague, presented her with a cut glass vase as a token of appreciation, which became a prized possession.

Barbara Ann was followed everywhere she went in Prague. One young man, thinking she was rich because she was famous, begged her to buy him a motorcycle.

Dick Button made history as the first American man to win the European title in Prague. He later recalled, "Barbara Ann and I shared many delightful times in Europe and America. Newsmen all over the world tried to drum up gossip for their columns by urging us to fall in love. The standard request after we both had won in a tournament was for a kissing picture which invariably appeared in print under the identical caption: 'Champion Kisses Champion'."

Tensions leading to the Communist Party coup d'état of Czechoslovakia's government were swelling just as the Championships were finishing. Barbara Ann, Mary, Margaret, Mr. Galbraith and Dick Button were lucky enough to leave Prague right before the airport was shut down.

Their wild European adventure was just beginning.

7

"She produced her skilful and artistic expression of skating art as if from out of a box in which everything was perfectly packed and orderly. She portrayed the almost perfect picture of the accepted idea of pre-war skating aims with just one difference. Her polish in execution gave it a new lustre, a modern finish." - Nigel Brown

After heading back to Davos to train at the Belvedere Hotel's private rink for a couple of weeks, Barbara Ann, Mary, Margaret and Mr. Galbraith made their way to St. Moritz for the big moment – the 1948 Winter Olympic Games.

The sun shone brightly in the idyllic town in the Swiss Alps when the women took to the ice to skate their compulsory figures. Dressed in a white wool and doeskin dress, pearls, woollen mittens and a bonnet embroidered with colourful flowers tied under her chin, Barbara Ann was so focused on the task at hand that she didn't even notice when a helicopter flew quite low over her. When Mr. Galbraith asked if it affected her concentration, she answered, "What helicopter?"

Before the lunch break, the ice began to melt. Swiss journalist Nigel Brown recalled, "The last ten skaters had to skate their counters under extremely difficult conditions... It was almost impossible for the last competitor to get round her figure, so 'sugary' had the ice become." The referee and judges met and decided that ice conditions were too poor to continue, and the competition was postponed until seven o'clock the next morning. The warm Foehn wind blew all night long and as the ice conditions hadn't improved, it was decided to postpone the figures for another day. The second night the wind changed direction and on the third morning, there was a cool breeze from the north and it was decided ice conditions were reasonable enough to continue. After all of the figures were skated, Barbara Ann had a sixteen-point lead over Jeannette Altwegg, Eva Pawlik and Jiřina Nekolová. To the surprise of many, Gretchen Van Zandt Merrill finished only sixth. Remarking on Barbara Ann's figures, Gretchen's coach Maribel Vinson Owen said, "Though her figures are not compass drawn or even comparable to Sonja Henie at her peak, she is like Sonja in that she is a cool customer when the pressure is on... She skated large powerful figures with calm assurance which made them look even better than they were."

During the figures, Mr. Galbraith had picked up on one of Jeannette Altwegg's bad habits and turned it into an opportunity. Barbara Ann recalled, "The ice surface we used was surrounded by snowbanks. Jeanette's coach [Jacques Gerschwiler] had a habit of standing at the side and extending a foot in the snow, close to the ice, so she'd have a target to line up her loops and keep them straight. It was a good idea but Sheldon picked up on it. He'd wait until she'd started a figure and then go stand beside her coach and stick out a foot not far from his. When she'd turn, she couldn't look up to see which foot it was she was supposed to be guided by. All she could see was two of them. By the time we'd done the six figures, she was pretty mixed up."

The ice conditions for the free skating were worse than they were for the figures. Three hockey games had been played on the ice before the competition, and it wasn't flooded because it would have turned into slush due to the temperature. The rink's workers shovelled away the snow that they could, but the ice was still extremely soft. Before the competition started, Barbara Ann and Mr. Galbraith surveyed the rink, noting the worst spots, and changed her program on the fly to avoid jumping in those problem areas. Though it wouldn't compute to skaters today, terrible ice conditions were a harsh reality in the days before Zambonis were a thing.

Barbara Ann wore a silver and white Karakul and broad tail dress for her free skating performance, designed by Toronto furrier Harry Springer. The dress almost did not make it to Switzerland. Mr. Springer had bought the furs down in New York and when he was crossing the border back into Canada, they were confiscated by border officials, due to new import restrictions. This caused a two-week delay and it had been down to the wire to get the dress ready in time for Barbara Ann's departure for Europe. In the lining of her dress, Springer and his workers signed their names, along with the message, "Good luck, Barbara Ann; Best Wishes; Toronto, 1947; We're Cheering For You!"

Considering the ice conditions, it's no wonder that few

of the women skated extremely well. In a show of good sportsmanship, American skater Eileen Seigh came into the dressing room after falling three times during her performance. She told Barbara Ann and the other skaters in the room about the bad ruts in the ice they should avoid. Unfortunately, no less than eleven competitors fell attempting the double loop jump. Gretchen Van Zandt Merrill's Olympic dream was shattered when she took two hard falls. Her choice of dress colour – gold – was perhaps a jinx.

You could hear a pin drop when Barbara Ann started her Olympic performance. Starting with three Axels in a row, she weaved her way through her program more cautiously than normal but demonstrated flawless technique, artistic flair and remarkable concentration. She never faltered. With a calculated and mesmerizing performance, Barbara Ann approached the pinnacle of perfection in the world of figure skating.

After her performance, Barbara Ann did a curious thing. Instead of hustling off to her dressing room, she stayed to applaud her fellow competitors. She wasn't standing there to psych them out, she genuinely wanted to cheer them on. That's how Canadians are.

When the marks were tallied, Barbara Ann was unanimously first on seven of the nine judge's scorecards. Eva Pawlik skated extremely well in the free skating and moved up to second and Jeannette Altwegg dropped to third. Gretchen Van Zandt Merrill ended the competition in a disastrous eighth and the

Czechoslovakian judge had her fifteenth. Canada's two other entries, Marilyn Ruth Take and Suzanne Morrow finished twelfth and fourteenth.

It bears mentioning that judging was very nationalistic and political in those days. The British judge had Jeannette Altwegg first, although she finished only sixth in free skating. Adolf Rosdol, the Austrian judge who gave first-place marks to Eva Pawlik, was suspended years later for instructing Austrian judges to communicate to other country's judges where to place skaters by giving hand signals. Canada's judge was Melville Rogers, the man who had coached Barbara Ann when the Minto Skating Club was without a professional and helped organize the fundraising campaign to send her to the Olympics. Though this was undoubtedly a conflict of interest, the Canadian Figure Skating Association was not by any means a skating organization with much pull at all in 1948, as compared to the skating federations of Europe, so having one judge in her corner was not necessarily a bad thing. Here are just a few of the examples of nationalistic judging at the 1948 Olympics:

American judge - had an American skater 5th, she finished 8th
Swiss judge - had a Swiss skater 10th, she finished 15th
British judge - had a British skater 1st, she finished 3rd
Canadian judge - had a Canadian skater 9th, she finished 14th
Austrian judge - had an Austrian skater 1st, she finished 2nd
French judge - had a French skater 9th, she finished 16th
Hungarian judge - had a Hungarian skater 8th, she finished 17th

Czechoslovakian judge - had Czechoslovakian skaters 2nd and 3rd, they finished 4th and 5th

After it was announced that Barbara Ann won, Reg Schroeder and Ab Renaud, Canadian hockey stars with the upset RCAF Flyers team, hoisted her up on their shoulders for photographers. In a newsreel video that was taken, she sincerely said, "Give my love to Canada and thank them for pulling for me."

Barbara Ann's win was a historic one. She was the first Canadian woman to win a gold medal in any sport at the Winter Olympics and the first North American woman to win an Olympic gold medal in figure skating. When she stood atop a makeshift wooden podium, in the middle of a blizzard between hockey periods, she heard "O Canada" play and saw the red and white flag flying. It was an incredibly moving moment. She remembered something that her late father Clyde had always told her: "Canada must always come first and if there's anything you can do for Canada, you must."

The day Barbara Ann won the Olympic gold medal, Prime Minister William Lyon Mackenzie King wrote in his diary, "I do not think there is any single individual whose life and art and talent has been watched as closely by the Canadian people as Barbara Ann Scott, or who has brought as much of a thrill to the entire nation and she has in what she has achieved, and the way in which she carried her Honours."

Jim Proudfoot later beautifully said, "Wayne Gretzky thinks he's idolized today, and he certainly is. But he doesn't know the half of it. In 1948, when Barbara Ann was Canada's Sweetheart, the nation's affection knew no bounds. The love was total and unreserved. Everybody wanted to be her brother or her sister, her father or mother or her boyfriend. There were no abstainers."

8

"If she is ever nervous before a championship contest, she never shows it." - Melville Rogers

Barbara Ann, Mary, Margaret and Mr. Galbraith returned to Davos on February 9, 1948, for the World Figure Skating Championships. While watching a hockey game between the Davos team and the British Olympic team before the competition, she discovered that the ice conditions were just as bad as they were in St. Moritz. Six feet of snow had fallen in the week leading up to the competition and locals said that it was the worst snowfall in fifty years. The warm temperatures, coupled with the snow, made for soft ice. It was nearly impossible for skaters to see their tracings when they did their figures. The ice conditions were the worst they had been in years at the World Championships. Former Olympic Medallist Theresa Weld Blanchard remarked, "The ice was not so much frozen water as frozen snow, and bad as it was in St. Moritz, it was far worse here."

The compulsory figures were paused twice due to the ice conditions. When they finally resumed, the judges had to judge the skaters almost entirely by what they saw as each figure was skated, because the tracings on the ice were so faint. When the marks were tallied, Barbara Ann had a narrow lead over Jeannette Altwegg, Eva Pawlik, Jiřína Nekolová and Ája Zanová. After her disastrous showing in St. Moritz, Gretchen Van Zandt Merrill decided not to compete, saying she was "over-trained and overtired".

The free skating was held almost immediately after the final figures were skated, on the main rink near the clubhouse where the ice was in slightly better condition. Barbara Ann wore a tailored white brocade dress, patterned with pink, green and silver, and skated her program to "Babes in Toyland", "Beautiful Island of Somewhere" and "Giselle" more conservatively than she had at the Olympics. With first-place marks from seven of the nine judges, she defended her World title. Austria's Eva Pawlik skated very well and was a crowd favourite, earning first-place marks from the Austrian and Hungarian judges. Jeannette Altwegg had a disappointing performance and dropped to fourth behind Jiřína Nekolová.

After the World Championships, Barbara Ann went on a whirlwind tour of Europe, giving an exhausting series of exhibitions in Oslo, Copenhagen, Paris, Bern, Vienna, Budapest, Garmisch-Partenkirchen and London. In Montchoisi, near Bern, she passed Switzerland's Gold Medal test, earning the highest marks ever achieved. Twenty thousand people came out to see her skate in Paris during the intermission of a hockey game. In London, she was invited to Madame Tussaud's to have her measurements taken for a waxwork figure. The only other figure skater to be featured at the famous Waxworks was British star Cecilia Colledge.

Before attending a reception at Canada House, Barbara

Ann received a royal invitation to have a private audience and tea at Buckingham Palace with Princess Elizabeth (later Queen Elizabeth II). Barbara Ann and the Princess talked about horseback riding and skating. The Princess had learned to skate as a young girl on the balcony rink at the Park Lane Ice Rink at Grosvenor House in London.

The Princess had read that Barbara Ann was very interested in seeing her wedding dress, and she arranged for an aide to show Barbara Ann and Mary through St. James's Place to see her dress and wedding gifts. Barbara Ann recalled, "It was a wonderful thrill to meet someone I had read about, seen pictures of, and heard about for so long... Then to find out she was so sweet, so nice!"

Barbara Ann, Mary, Margaret and Mr. Galbraith's transatlantic flight back to Canada was an hour and a half late leaving because cargo had to be removed and repacked to accommodate for the party's extra luggage, which was three hundred pounds overweight. The plane was supposed to have landed in Gander, Newfoundland, but the plane was diverted to Sydney, Nova Scotia. As it turned out, five thousand Cape Bretoners had waited for nine hours in the snow to catch a glimpse of the Queen of the Ice at two in the morning. A sleepy Barbara Ann came out to greet the crowd and shook hands with a brawny coal miner, who reached across the plane's ramp and said, "Come give us a hand, Babs!"

After a short flight from Sydney to the Dorval Airport in Montreal, Barbara Ann, Mary, Margaret and Mr.

Galbraith travelled by train to Ottawa on March 9, 1948.

An estimated one hundred and fifty thousand people – two-thirds of the population of Ottawa and Hull – came out to cheer on Barbara Ann that day at the old Union Station, Confederation Square and the surrounding streets. Children were given a half-day at school to attend. Traffic was at a standstill. One hundred and twenty-five city police and sixteen Mounties on horses served as security. The police station displayed a large round sign that said "Welcome home Barbara Ann - Ottawa's Sweetheart". People in the crowd held homemade banners that simply said, "We love you."

Prime Minister William Lyon Mackenzie King and Mayor Stanley Lewis greeted Barbara Ann's train at the station. The Prime Minister welcomed Barbara Ann, Mary, Margaret and Mr. Galbraith back to Canada and spoke of how proud the entire country was of Barbara Ann. As her daffodil-covered car drove through the streets of Ottawa, the crowd chanted "All hail Queen Barbara!" After the Parade ended, there was a civic reception, where Mayor Lewis gave Barbara Ann a gold key to the city and she was made the first 'Freewoman of the City of Ottawa. The only other skater to have been given the key to the city was Cecilia Colledge, before the War when she came to perform at the Minto Follies. Barbara Ann remembered, "People were so kind and nice. It was sort of like I was their little girl and they were my big family."

In his diary, the Prime Minister recalled his speech at the

reception that day: "This reception in the Capital of Canada symbolized the feeling of all Canada toward her and the honour she had done herself. Done our country. I then said how we had followed with interest from the time she left in December until her return. Marvelled at the endurance of travel by air, train, meetings with [the] public, photographers etc. I said I had thought a general election was quite a task in that respect but it seemed to be nothing compared to what she had seen and done in foreign countries. I then told her that she had spoken of the cables that I had sent. I never remembered sending so many cables to one person in so short a time. All of them related to a great event in the life of a nation. Said that M.P.s had greatly enthused over messages sent on behalf of the country and the people. Wanted her to know they had all been printed in Ransard and remain for all time as part of the records of Canada and the pride we had in her and her achievements... I would like to speak of her part in the international arena of world affairs. Times we were in were very unsettling. People's minds were anxious and the like but she shone forth in her triumphs as a bright star in a troubled world. She helped to bring cheer and brightness. Helped to strengthen the wills of others as well as her own."

Barbara Ann and Mary were even taken down onto the floor at the House of Commons, while Parliament was in session. It was a great honour, particularly because many of the Members of Parliament had been friends with Barbara Ann's father Clyde.

The Prime Minister gave considerable thought to

making Barbara Ann the first recipient of the Canada Medal, which had been created as the highest award that civilians and military personnel could receive. He decided against it after receiving a letter from a woman from Brandon, Manitoba, saying that the Medal should be reserved for war heroes and great Canadians like Frederick Banting, who invented insulin. The Canada Medal was ultimately never awarded.

After being fêted in Ottawa, Barbara Ann, Mary and Mr. Galbraith flew to Malton Airport in Toronto in *The Globe and Mail*'s plane for another homecoming parade. They were met at the airport by Mayor Hiram E. McCallum and his wife Margaret. Canadian and North American Champion Ralph McCreath, who Barbara Ann called "Tarzan" because he wore leopard-printed swimming trunks, drove them from the King Edward Hotel to City Hall in a cream-coloured convertible. Pipe and brass bands played and Mounties on horseback galloped past. Afterwards, there was a dinner dance in the Crystal Ballroom at the King Edward Hotel. Barbara Ann was presented with the very prestigious Lou E. Marsh Memorial Trophy for the third time, which was a record.

Barbara Ann had a Toronto policeman guarding her suite at the hotel from enthusiastic fans. While she was resting in her room, she heard a knock on the door. The policeman sternly told her, "You haven't ordered any dinner, Miss Scott. It's getting late, and you can't go without nourishment. We've got to look after you." She told him she wasn't hungry, but he picked up her phone and ordered tea anyway.

This well-meaning policeman had caught onto something that Barbara Ann never attempted to hide. She never gave much thought to her diet and often skipped breakfast and lunch. She didn't even eat turkey at Christmas time, because she believed "if you eat a heavy meal, you can't skate well." She lived on a diet of eggs, vegetables, milk, orange juice and cheese. She didn't like steak, but she ate it from time to time. She wasn't a lover of tea or coffee and she didn't have much of a sweet tooth, though she would occasionally have a hot sundae as a treat. She never smoked and avoided hard liquor.

At receptions, Barbara Ann would take a tiny sip of champagne and then "get rid of the glass as gracefully as possible." She recalled, "In Sweden, there is a rather horrible drink called schnapps which is made out of, of all things, caraway seeds and which is guaranteed to inflame any throat after one sip. They serve it in liqueur glasses and are forever toasting each other with it. Well, they think you're an awful pill if you don't join them in a toast, so I have... stood with many a glass of schnapps in my hand, touching it to my lips and then putting it down again. No one ever seems to wonder why my glass never empties."

At five foot three and ninety-seven pounds, Barbara Ann was very much underweight by today's BMI standards. She was an incredible role model for thousands of young women growing up in Canada, but it is absolutely worth recognizing that her diet and weight inadvertently set an unachievable and unhealthy example for Canadians.

9

"I am grateful... for all Ottawa did for me, all they gave to me, all they helped me... In a way, I think you could say that Ottawa is the love of my life." - Barbara Ann Scott

Before Barbara Ann even stepped foot in Canada, carnivals with her as the headliner in Toronto, Ottawa and Montreal had sold out. Five skaters posed for a press photo advertising the Toronto Skating Club's carnival at Maple Leaf Gardens, holding a sign that said: "Sorry, We're All Sold Out". One was a very young Frances Dafoe, who would later win the gold medal in pairs skating at the 1954 and 1955 World Figure Skating Championships and become a close friend of Barbara Ann's.

When tickets went on sale for another carnival featuring Barbara Ann in Brandon, Manitoba, people lined up for four hours at the ticket wicket and one woman fainted from the crush of the line. One lucky eight-year-old boy got to attend the Toronto Carnival at the last minute and meet Barbara Ann. She and her mother told organizers to give an extra ticket for a seat in their private box to "the most deserving child looking in from outside."

If Barbara Ann so much as sneezed in the spring of 1948, Ottawa's two daily newspapers – the *Citizen* and *Journal*, wrote a story about it, and news about Barbara Ann wasn't relegated to the Sports pages. It was front-page material. She was interviewed on Foster Hewitt's popular radio program Canadian Cavalcade. Cay Moore, the Royal York Hotel's social hostess, wrote a book about her called *She Skated Into Our Hearts*, which respected sports historian Don Morrow later dismissed as "fictionalized drivel". Barbara Ann mania was at such a peak across Canada that a minister in Woodstock even made her the subject of his sermon at a Sunday church service.

There was always speculation about her love life. George Fulford Jr., the son of a Liberal Member of Parliament from Brockville, gave her a ring as a friendship gift, which she promptly returned because everyone kept inferring she was engaged to him. One gossip columnist suggested she was seriously dating actor Kirk Douglas. "People are always thinking and saying I'm engaged if they see me with a boy," lamented Barbara Ann. "Then they phone Mother to ask about it. She's heard it so often she usually asks right at the start of the conversation: 'Who's Barb engaged to now?'"

Not everyone was thrilled with her image or the attention she was receiving. A Quebec Roman Catholic newspaper accused her of encouraging "provocative poses and indecent costumes on the rink... Let us ask ourselves why our girls who take up fancy figure skating are lacking in modesty. Is it the custom to make use of sex appeal to attract crowds to rinks, as well as to picture shows?"

In late March, Barbara Ann travelled to the Glencoe

Club in Calgary for what would be her final competition – the 1948 Canadian Figure Skating Championships. It was the first time that the Canadian Championships were held west of Winnipeg.

Barbara Ann skated much better in Calgary than she had at the Olympics or World Championships and easily won her fourth and final Canadian senior ladies title. Six thousand spectators cheered her on at the Glencoe Club that year and she received a perfect mark from judge A.L. Dysart of Winnipeg. It was believed to be the first perfect mark of 10.0 ever awarded at the Canadian Championships at the time.

The following month, she starred in the Minto Follies in Ottawa, which toured to other skating clubs in the district. Over one hundred thousand people in total saw the shows that year. Afterwards, Barbara Ann presented a new Barbara Ann Scott Trophy to Pierrette Paquin and a new Colonel Clyde Scott Trophy to Donald Tobin. The regiment her late father belonged to donated both trophies to Minto Skating Club, with the understanding that they were awarded to the Ottawa skaters who achieved the highest honours at the Canadian Championships each year. Paquin went on to make history as the first Canadian woman to serve as a judge at the World Figure Skating Championships in 1957.

In May, Barbara Ann received an invitation from Bess Truman, the First Lady of the United States, to carry golf clubs in a charity golf tournament between Bing Crosby and Bob Hope in Washington, D.C. She ended up being Bing Crosby's "honorary scorekeeper". The next day, Barbara Ann and Dick Button were invited to meet President Harry S. Truman at The White House. Dick Button later recalled, "Mr. Truman put us at ease immediately, despite a formidable barrage of newsreel cameras and the chilling formality preceding the ceremony, by presenting us with pens inscribed: 'I swiped this from Harry S. Truman'."

In Ottawa, Mayor Stanley Lewis announced that the famous convertible Barbara Ann had to return the year prior was being repainted in powder blue, her favourite colour. It was given back to her with a new license plate - "48-U1". Acceptance of the car didn't automatically mean she was turning professional, as the Canadian Figure Skating Association had crossed their T's and dotted their I's to ensure that proper approvals were given.

Barbara Ann drove her new ride to Brockville, and then to a cottage in the Laurentians for a short holiday. She had a lot to think about. She weighed the options of remaining amateur, turning professional and skating in shows or putting her skates away entirely and going to McGill University to study domestic science. Mary told an inquisitive reporter, "I want to get her into a pair of slacks and see her relax in a hammock, with nothing on her mind but clear, calm consideration of the future. She will make her own decision, for it is her life she will be leading."

The whole time Barbara Ann was on vacation, reporters

hounded her about when she planned to cash in on her stardom. She told one reporter, "As somebody once said, money isn't everything, you know. I don't want to sound corny, but it's happiness, first and foremost, that I want out of life."

Gossip of Hollywood offers swirled, with *The Globe and Mail* reporting that a seventy-five hundred dollar a week contract for a film was on the table. Mary rebuffed the rumour. "Barbara Ann is not considering any contracts," she said. "She considers herself a good Canadian but she sees no reason why she should work terribly hard and then have to turn most of her earnings over to the government."

Finally, on October 11, 1948, Barbara Ann officially announced her decision. She was turning professional.

Barbara Ann Scott. Photo courtesy Toronto Public Library, Toronto Star Photograph Archive. Rights: Public domain.

Barbara Ann Scott holding a baby. Photo courtesy Cloyne and District Historical Society - Alkenbrack Family Album. Used with permission.

Barbara Ann Scott (back), Mary Scott and Sheldon Galbraith (front). Photo courtesy City of Toronto Archives. Rights: Public domain.

Barbara Ann Scott. Photo courtesy Toronto Public Library, Toronto Star Photograph Archive. Rights: Public domain.

Barbara Ann Scott and Jimmy Grogan. Photo courtesy BAnQ: Bibliothèque et Archives nationales du Québec. Rights: Public domain.

John E. Morrison and Mary Scott. Barbara Ann Scott. Photo courtesy BAnQ: Bibliothèque et Archives nationales du Québec. Rights: Public domain.

Dick Button and Barbara Ann Scott. Barbara Ann Scott. Photo courtesy BAnQ: Bibliothèque et Archives nationales du Québec. Rights: Public domain.

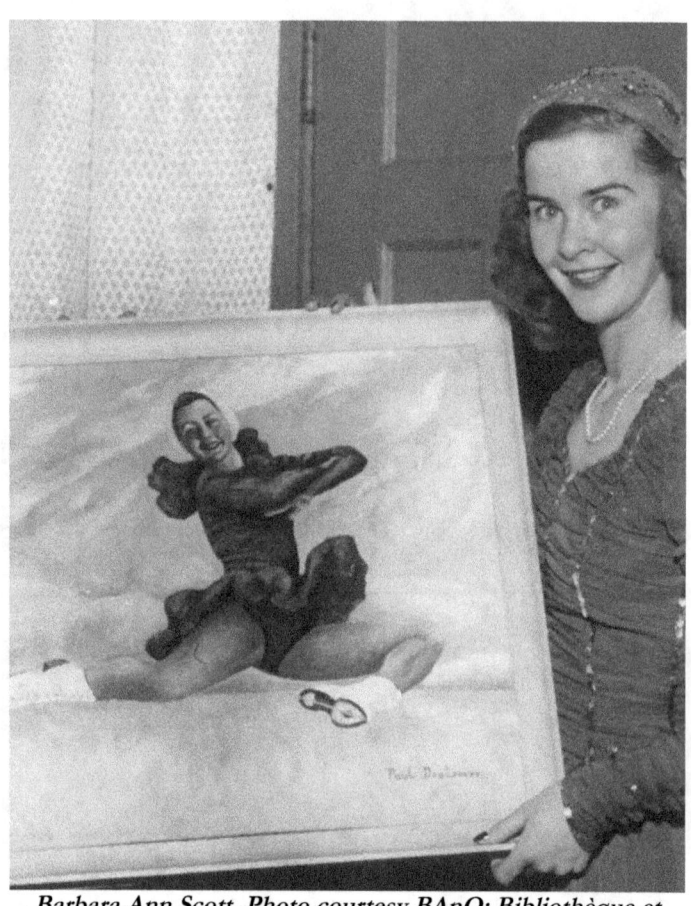

Barbara Ann Scott. Photo courtesy BAnQ: Bibliothèque et Archives nationales du Québec. Rights: Public domain.

Barbara Ann Scott. Photo courtesy Cloyne and District Historical Society - Alkenbrack Family Album. Used with permission.

*Barbara Ann Scott, Geoffrey Caldwell and Mary Scott.
Photo courtesy Cloyne and District Historical Society -
Alkenbrack Family Album. Used with permission.*

Barbara Ann Scott. Photo courtesy City of Toronto Archives. Rights: Public domain.

Barbara Ann Scott. Photo courtesy BAnQ: Bibliothèque et Archives nationales du Québec. Rights: Public domain.

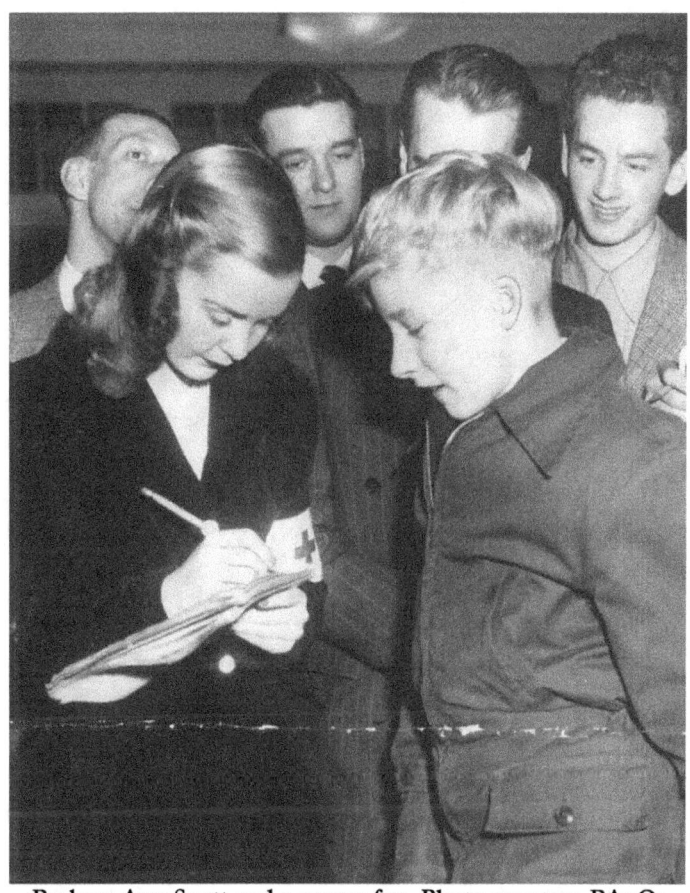

Barbara Ann Scott and a young fan. Photo courtesy BAnQ: Bibliothèque et Archives nationales du Québec. Rights: Public domain.

Barbara Ann Scott. Photo courtesy BAnQ: Bibliothèque et Archives nationales du Québec. Rights: Public domain.

Barbara Ann Scott. Photo courtesy BAnQ: Bibliothèque et Archives nationales du Québec. Rights: Public domain.

Mary Scott, Sheldon Galbraith and Barbara Ann Scott. Photo courtesy BAnQ: Bibliothèque et Archives nationales du Québec. Rights: Public domain.

Barbara Ann Scott. Photo courtesy BAnQ: Bibliothèque et Archives nationales du Québec. Rights: Public domain.

Barbara Ann Scott. Photo courtesy BAnQ: Bibliothèque et Archives nationales du Québec. Rights: Public domain.

Barbara Ann Scott. Photo courtesy of the Boston Public Library, Leslie Jones Collection. Used with permission.

Barbara Ann Scott. Photo courtesy of the Boston Public Library, Leslie Jones Collection. Used with permission.

Barbara Ann Scott. Photo courtesy BAnQ: Bibliothèque et Archives nationales du Québec. Rights: Public domain.

Barbara Ann Scott. Photo courtesy BAnQ: Bibliothèque et Archives nationales du Québec. Rights: Public domain.

Barbara Ann Scott. Photo courtesy BAnQ: Bibliothèque et Archives nationales du Québec. Rights: Public domain.

Barbara Ann Scott. Photo courtesy BAnQ: Bibliothèque et Archives nationales du Québec. Rights: Public domain.

Mary Scott and Barbara Ann Scott. Photo courtesy BAnQ: Bibliothèque et Archives nationales du Québec. Rights: Public domain.

Barbara Ann Scott. Photo courtesy BAnQ: Bibliothèque et Archives nationales du Québec. Rights: Public domain.

Barbara Ann Scott and Mary Scott. Photo courtesy BAnQ: Bibliothèque et Archives nationales du Québec. Rights: Public domain.

Barbara Ann Scott and Dick Button. Photo courtesy BAnQ: Bibliothèque et Archives nationales du Québec. Rights: Public domain.

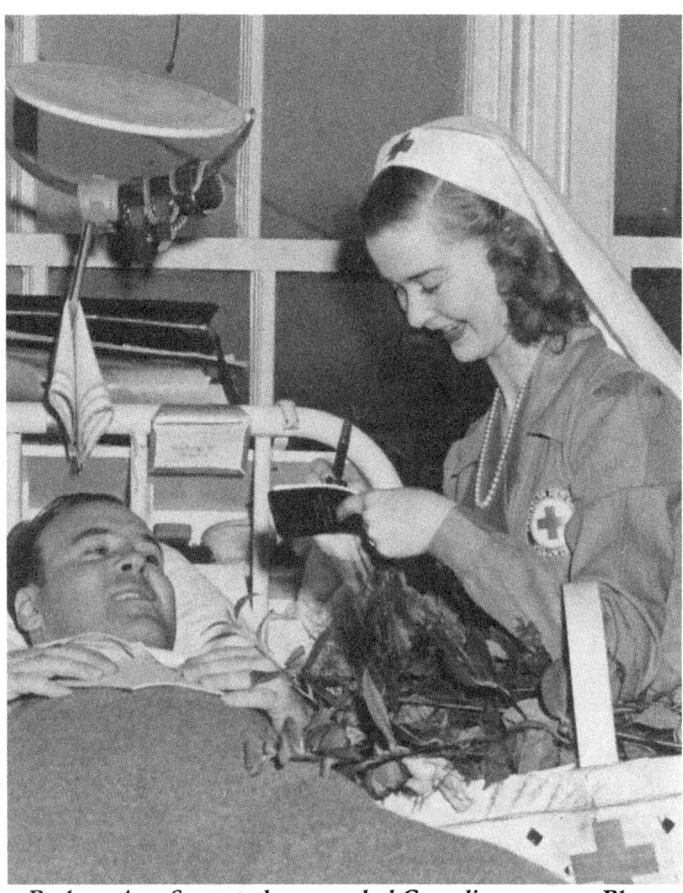

Barbara Ann Scott and a wounded Canadian veteran. Photo courtesy BAnQ: Bibliothèque et Archives nationales du Québec. Rights: Public domain.

Barbara Ann Scott. Photo courtesy BAnQ: Bibliothèque et Archives nationales du Québec. Rights: Public domain.

Barbara Ann Scott, Donald B. Cruikshank and Mary Scott. Photo courtesy BAnQ: Bibliothèque et Archives nationales du Québec. Rights: Public domain.

Barbara Ann Scott. Photo courtesy BAnQ: Bibliothèque et Archives nationales du Québec. Rights: Public domain.

Barbara Ann Scott. Photo courtesy BAnQ: Bibliothèque et Archives nationales du Québec. Rights: Public domain.

Barbara Ann Scott dolls. Photo courtesy Yvonne Butorac. Used with permission.

Audience at Barbara Ann Scott's homecoming parade. Photo courtesy Skate Canada Archive. Used with permission.

Michael Kirby and Barbara Ann Scott. Photo courtesy Skate Canada Archive. Used with permission.

Barbara Ann Scott at the 1948 Winter Olympics. Photo courtesy Skate Canada Archive. Used with permission.

Barbara Ann Scott. Photo courtesy Skate Canada Archive. Used with permission.

Barbara Ann Scott. Photo courtesy Skate Canada Archive. Used with permission.

Barbara Ann Scott. Photo courtesy Skate Canada Archive. Used with permission.

Barbara Ann Scott. Photo courtesy Skate Canada Archive. Used with permission.

Barbara Ann Scott and Tommy King. Photo courtesy Skate Canada Archive. Used with permission.

Barbara Ann Scott. Photo courtesy Skate Canada Archive. Used with permission.

Barbara Ann Scott and Tommy King. Photo courtesy Skate Canada Archive. Used with permission.

Barbara Ann Scott. Photo courtesy Skate Canada Archive. Used with permission.

Barbara Ann Scott and Tommy King. Photo courtesy Skate Canada Archive. Used with permission.

Barbara Ann Scott and Tommy King. Photo courtesy Skate Canada Archive. Used with permission.

10

"When you smile at the audience, they smile right back." -
Barbara Ann Scott

Barbara Ann's decision to turn professional was not made lightly. She had already achieved her goals of winning the Canadian, North American, European, World and Olympic titles, and at the age of twenty, didn't see any reason to continue doing "the same things over and over again." She knew that she wanted to help less fortunate people, and at the same time, alleviate the financial burden on her widowed mother Mary.

After careful consideration and many discussions with Mary and her late father Clyde's friends, a plan was devised to set up a charitable organization, which would serve as Barbara Ann's employer.

The St. Lawrence Foundation to Aid Crippled Children paid Barbara Ann an allowance, which covered her and Mary's expenses. Ten percent of her earnings went to her representative, MCA (Music Corporation of America). Her agents Morris M. Schrier and George B. Evans also received a cut. The Foundation then administered donations to charity on her behalf. She never received a paycheck beyond her allowance.

The Foundation consisted of Toronto lawyer J.S.D. Tory, Robert V. Hicks, a lawyer in Tory's firm, Charles F.

Lindsay, a banker and friend of Barbara Ann's father Clyde and H.H. Caldwell of the Caldwell linen mills in Prescott. The Caldwell and Scott families had been very close friends for many years. H.H.'s daughter Betty stayed with the Scotts when she was going to school in Ottawa and frequently travelled with Barbara Ann. As youngsters, Barbara Ann, Betty and her brother Geoff played together and swam and boated at the Caldwell's luxurious home on the banks of the St. Lawrence River in Prescott. It was fitting that the Caldwell family had a stake in her future because they had been an important part of her young life.

It was decided that Barbara Ann's big professional debut would take place on December 22, 1948, at Twentieth Century-Fox's Roxy Theatre on Broadway in New York City. Barbara Ann made a trip to New York City to see the theatre's tank ice stage and be measured for costumes. While there, she visited the Stork Club, 21 Club and the Starlight Roof. She also saw the Broadway musical *High Button Shoes* and went backstage to meet the show's leading man Phil Silvers.

Upon her return to Ottawa, a 32 X 40-inch section of ice - the same size as the Roxy Theatre's stage - was roped off at the Minto Skating Club, so Barbara Ann could practice. She worked with Melville Rogers to adapt her programs to a smaller ice surface. A week before she left Ottawa by train for New York City, Twentieth Century-Fox cameramen arrived to take publicity photographs. She had lunch with former Prime Minister William Lyon MacKenzie King and the new Prime

Minister Louis St. Laurent. The Minto Skating Club threw her a big send-off party and gave her a hot water jug which matched a silver set the Club had started for her when she first won the North American Figure Skating Championships in 1945. Barbara Ann recalled, "Things got pretty hectic when we were ready to leave Ottawa. As usual, I'd left everything to the last minute. I hadn't even done my Christmas shopping, and we had 300 cards to send off. Then we had to pack. It gets a little complicated when you try to sort out what you'll need for two months. When we got through we had 14 suitcases, and we really didn't have many clothes. The trouble was I had two pair of skates and boots and I had to take all of my mascots. They're my elephants and my Swedish lucky man, and Junior, my Koala. When we had to change trains in Montreal, the Customs man looked at all the luggage and just groaned. Poor man - he had to go through every case. Grand Central Station looked like a movie set when we got in. Lights everywhere, and cameras. Col. Bennett came down to meet me for Mayor O'Dwyer, and I had to make a speech. I couldn't think of anything except to thank him for coming down without any breakfast."

More than five thousand New Yorkers and a large contingent of Canadians lined up outside the Roxy Theatre on December 22, 1948, for Barbara Ann's professional debut. The show had a winter carnival theme and the programs she skated were "Babes in Toyland" and "Ave Maria".

"It was something like going into a competition,"

remembered Barbara Ann. "I had the same butterfly feeling in my tummy, as though I had to go out to win. But something that happened just before my entrance made me know that everything was going to be all right. One of the men who pulled the sleigh is a real old-timer in show business. He gave my hand a squeeze and I knew everything was going to be fine. And so it was, too, once I started to skate."

When Barbara Ann went backstage after her performance, her dressing room was filled to the brim with flowers. A large bouquet of white tulips caught her eye and she was shocked to see what was written on the card: "The best, always, Sonja Henie."

After opening night, she was taken to the Canadian Club at the Waldorf Astoria Hotel by limousine. Rather than champagne and caviar, she ordered a sandwich and a glass of milk. "When I ordered milk, they just gaped at me," she later laughed. "They wouldn't believe me at first. They finally produced the milk but it took them a long, long time. Then they stood and watched me drink it. What's wrong with drinking milk?" After finishing her milk, she received an unusual and lavish gift. Hon. Hugh D. Scully, Canada's Consul General, presented her with a pair of skates made of palladium, a precious metal even more expensive than gold. The custom-made skates, manufactured in Weston, Ontario, were estimated to be worth five thousand dollars. They were believed to be the most expensive pair of skates in the world at the time.

Papers from Halifax to Vancouver covered Barbara Ann's professional debut daily, and *The Globe and Mail* and *Montreal Standard* sent reporters to New York City to cover the story. The *Medicine Hat Daily News* gave Barbara Ann a whole page in its Christmas issue. Though the audience loved her, it was clear from the beginning that the adjustment from the amateur world to the professional scene was challenging. During the four to five-week engagement, she skated up to five shows a day – six on Saturdays - even on Christmas Day. On Boxing Day, she had to perform at midnight. On the morning of New Year's Day, only a handful of people showed up because they were all hung over.

Barbara Ann despised the pancake cosmetics that her hair and make-up man, Ernie Adler, put on her. When she insisted he didn't make her lips so big or her eyebrows so dark, he huffed, "What that girl doesn't know about theatre could fill a book. I'll have to help her quite a while yet. She hasn't come up the harsh way that teaches you what's what, like the rest of us." Adler later did Judy Garland's hair for her Broadway shows.

Barbara Ann's first paycheck as a professional was for about eighty thousand dollars, but it went right to the Foundation. "It isn't the way I was told it would be at all," she told one reporter. "I'd heard when I turned professional that I'd meet a lot of cold, hard people who just wanted to get something out of me. I haven't met a single person like that." Among the nice people she got to meet were baseball legends Jackie Robinson and Joe DiMaggio.

Barbara Ann continued to be tremendously popular in Canada when she was in New York City. So many people took up the sport because of her that the Canadian Figure Skating Association's membership numbers almost doubled. Officials in London, Ontario reported that in 1948, Barbara Ann and Barbara were among the most popular baby names in the city. Thirty-five babies had been named Barbara Ann and another fifty-eight Barbara.

Hundreds of poems were written about her by young people from coast to coast. This verse written by Jill Hodgkin, a Toronto boarding school student, was one of the most charming:

Barbara Ann Scott!
Artistry never equalled before,
Rhythm on an icy floor,
Beauty with her flashing blades,
Ambition hers that never fades,
Radiant charm with happy face,
Acrobat with perfect grace.

Attentiveness to all details,
Never slack and never fails.
Newspapers relate those tales.

Skillful in her chosen field,
Clever and not one to yield,
Ottawa's pride and joy!
To everyone she is, in truth,
The symbol of Canadian youth.

Across the country, people also made Barbara Ann Scott scrapbooks. Gloria Fordyce, who donated hers to the Skate Canada Archives at Barbara Ann's suggestion recalled, "I started collecting every story and picture I could find on her. When one of her pictures would appear in the paper I would write and order a reprint and pay for it out of my allowance."

Department stores cashed in on her popularity every chance they could get. Simpsons sold a line of Barbara Ann Scott sportswear, including a wool Jacquard-style sweater in her favourite colour – powder blue. Eaton's carried white, red and blue headscarves with Barbara Ann's picture and autograph for a dollar and fifty cents a pop. Sears stocked Barbara Ann Scott skates, with "white elk top-grain uppers and chromed Sheffield steel blades". The most famous collectible was the Barbara Ann Scott Doll.

The Barbara Ann Scott Doll was designed by the Reliable Toy Company and was inspired by the Madame Alexander dolls of Sonja Henie and Shirley Temple, which were designed by Lipfert. Made out of a fragile composition, the doll came with pairs of shoes and skates and a letter from Barbara Ann. When it first came out, the doll cost just under six dollars in the Eaton's catalogue. The doll was sold from 1948 to 1955, and every year it came with a different costume. It was the ultimate Christmas gift that youngsters wanted to find under the tree, but Barbara Ann was never a fan. Being very conscious of her body image, she didn't like the fact that the doll had a round tummy and thick legs.

"What an ugly little thing," she said many years later. "I've always hated it, with its ratty marabou around the bottom of the skirt... I'm always signing people's grandmother's dolls."

There was a certain irony to the fact that the doll was so popular, and Barbara Ann was not a fan of it. Throughout her entire career, journalists had treated her like a doll or a beauty queen on skates, rather than the talented elite athlete that she was. She was billed as a "Petite 18-Year Old Beauty", "Little Lady of the Graceful Blades" and "Ottawa's Own Pin-Up Girl". Sports historian Don Morrow criticized this hyper-fixation on her beauty: "Barely mentioned were her qualities of tenacity, self-sacrifice, determination, her lonely quest for excellence through thousands of practice hours as an athlete, a real person working towards admirable human achievement."

After the Roxy Theatre show ended, Barbara Ann went to Washington, D.C. The club's professional, former Canadian Champion Osborne Colson, collaborated with her on three new programs for performances on tank ice at the Chicago Theater and the Skating Club of Boston's Ice Chips show at Boston Garden. She made her first performance as a professional in Canada in Toronto on May 10, 1949, at the Rotary Club Ice Revue at Maple Leaf Gardens, backed by a fifty-piece orchestra and large choir. While in Toronto, she made a personal appearance at Simpsons, signing autographs for anyone who bought a Barbara Ann Scott doll. She celebrated her twenty-first birthday at a civic reception at Toronto's

City Hall. Mayor McCallum led fifteen hundred people in singing "Happy Birthday" to her. Afterward, Mary threw a buffet dinner at the Royal York Hotel, serving lobsters sent by friends in New Brunswick.

In the weeks that followed, Barbara Ann starred in the Minto Follies and the Granite Club's carnival and attended the North American Figure Skating Championships in Philadelphia, where her successor Marlene Smith won the silver medal.

Barbara Ann's rise to stardom came at a unique time. When she won the Olympic gold medal in 1948, there were less than three hundred and fifty television sets in Canada, but from 1948 to 1952, thousands more were sold. However, it wasn't television that first introduced many Canadians to her skating.

Newsreels of her skating were shown in theatres before movies, and two short films were released by the National Film Board of Canada. *An Introduction to the Art of Figure Skating* was an eleven-minute educational film on compulsory figures narrated by Melville Rogers, with a brief performance by Barbara Ann. *Dancing Blades*, also billed as *Beauty & The Blade* was a twelve-minute colour film featuring three performances by Barbara Ann.

These short films, which were seen by thousands, were rented out by mail to theatres and skating clubs across North America. They were also loaned out to people in over fifty countries abroad, through the Departments of External Affairs. Barbara Ann, as it turned out, was a big hit in Pakistan. Unfortunately, the Sri Lankans returned the films with a note that said the Sinhalese people weren't interested in ice skating because they had never seen ice.

In May of 1949, Barbara Ann was invited to be the guest of honour at the Newspaper Byline ball in Toronto. Before the event, she practised at the Granite Club and forgot her wallet in the dressing room. When she returned, it wasn't there. The empty wallet, which had contained more than two hundred dollars, was found in a mailbox near the club by post office officials.

This was just one of several unpleasant events that occurred after Barbara Ann became famous.

11

"I can't stand people who make a fuss and complain and make a rumpus about things. There is always a quiet way to deal with a problem." - Barbara Ann Scott

Barbara Ann's fame came with a price. Not only did the press pursue her relentlessly, they even published her address and phone number more than once. Over the years, she received many unsettling letters and phone calls.

A man from Germany asked Barbara Ann for money to buy a new house and a woman from northern Ontario wanted her to pay her mortgage. "Send me five thousand dollars. I know you have it," the woman wrote. She also received letters from religious fanatics who wanted to "save" her.

When Barbara Ann was skating at the Roxy Theatre in New York City, a man kept sending her orchids every single night. On one occasion, they were signed by 'The G-Man' and on another, they came with a note saying the man was with the RCAF and he wanted her to meet him at midnight at a hotel bar. She gave the flowers to an elevator operator who had a sick friend and tried to laugh it off.

On three separate occasions, things seriously escalated. During the summer of 1948, when Barbara Ann and

Mary were vacationing at a cottage near Brockville, a man started calling long distance and writing bizarre letters saying, "I got your message and you are the only person who can help me." After midnight on July 23, 1948, during a thunderstorm, the man tracked her down at the cottage and started pounding on the door yelling, "Is that you, Barbara Ann?" Mary stood behind the door with a toy baseball bat until the police arrived and apprehended him.

On August 7, 1949, Barbara Ann was travelling to the beach in Turkey Point and stopped to ask a man parked on the side of the road for directions. The man ended up following her to the beach, leaving at the same time she did and tailgating her. The situation made her so uncomfortable that the incident was reported to the police, but they dropped the charges with the warning that the man, a garage owner, was to stay away from her.

The most disturbing encounter occurred in February of 1951 when a tall, shabbily dressed thirty-two-year-old French Canadian man living in Toronto named Joseph Maconse showed up at the apartment Mary and Barbara Ann were renting. He rang all the doorbells in the apartment building and started shouting, "I must see Barbara Ann!"

The tenant who lived in the apartment above Mary and Barbara Ann came down to see who it was when his buzzer was pressed. Mr. Maconse tried to push his way past him. When the tenant who answered the door tried to stop him, he was grabbed by the throat and bitten on the arm. Mr. Maconse rushed past him and reached the door to Barbara Ann's apartment just as Mary opened it. Curiously, he yelled, "If you give me my money, I'll go."

Mr. Maconse got his foot inside the door, but a neighbour bopped him on the bean with her rolling pin. Five other neighbours sat on him in the hallway until the police showed up to apprehend him. He had been bothering Barbara Ann for quite some time, showing up at the apartment building once before and using "terrible language" when he was told she wasn't in. He had called her regularly, asking her to go out with him and threatening to "come and get her" if she didn't. He even showed up at the Toronto Skating Club trying to talk to her but was kicked out.

A week later, Mr. Maconse was formally charged with trespassing, forcible entry and threatening behaviour, and committed to a mental institution.

Barbara Ann's only comment on the incident was, "We had a rather unpleasant visitor."

12

"I've never worried about people liking me or not liking me because I've always liked them." - Barbara Ann Scott

In the autumn of 1949, Canada was at the height of Barbara Ann Scott fever. Though skating tours like the Ice Follies, Ice Capades and Ice Cycles had visited Canada numerous times and a small-scale production had been tried earlier that year in Ontario, a homegrown Trans-Canada large-scale skating revue had never been attempted. Who could have been better to headline a historic first than Barbara Ann?

The Skating Sensations of 1950 tour was the brainchild of Tommy Gorman, a founder of the NHL and seven-time winner of the Stanley Cup. Along with his son Frank and J.J. Walsh, Tommy co-ordinated the mammoth effort through the Ottawa-based firm National Sports Enterprise. A cast of sixty skaters was hired to complement Barbara Ann, including the St. Louis-based adagio pair Bob and Peggy White, Johnny Labrecque, Jerry Rehfield, comedians Johnny Melendez and Eddie Brandstetter and Puerto Rican skater Manuel del Toro. A live orchestra was also brought on board, conducted by Lloyd Cooper. Crooner Rudy Hanson served as vocalist and master of ceremonies.

Osborne Colson was the show's director and choreographer. Barbara Ann recalled, "Never have I met someone with so much patience. He is a perfect example of how to look cheerful when things go wrong. Never once in all our training time did I hear him speak a cross word to anyone, and that is quite something, especially when you consider that he did the choreography, training and costumes, helped with the individual numbers, and kept everybody happy." Mary was ever-present as were Barbara Ann's poodles Sambo and Scoop. Sambo had been given to her by members of the Toronto Men's Press Club.

The tour premiered on October 10, 1949, in Winnipeg, zigzagging its way across the country for close to eight months, playing over two hundred and twenty shows at over sixty memorial arenas. The tour had a gross profit of over eight hundred and fifty thousand dollars and was seen by more than one million people. Canada's population at the time was just under fourteen million.

Skating Sensations of 1950 didn't just play the same ten or so Canadian cities that we're accustomed to these days. It was a milk run of sorts, stopping to give one or two evening performances and a matinee in just about every community imaginable. "I went to every little town and village and skated," Barbara Ann recalled. "I wanted to do that for them."

Barbara Ann had fourteen costume changes during each show on the tour. She performed the "Danse Macabre", a Slavonic dance, a Chopin nocturne and a Spanish duet with Manuel del Toro, dressed in ostrich feathers. She dressed as a Southern belle in an adaptation of *Showboat* and starred in an on-ice version of *Goldilocks and The Three Bears*. One act that would not have aged well at all due to its blatant cultural appropriation was an "Indian Legend" act, where Barbara Ann donned a headdress and appeared as "Princess Shining Star".

Whose bright idea this was remains a mystery, but we do know that Barbara visited the Tsuut'ina Nation's reservation outside of Calgary after the 1948 Canadian Figure Skating Championships. At a ceremony, she was given the name "Shining Star" by Chief David Crowchild. Later, her "Princess Shining Star" costume was designed by Madeline Morigeau, a needlewoman from St. Mary's, a member community of the Ktunaxa Nation near Cranbrook. Did that make it right? Of course not. But it was 1949, and cultural sensitivity wasn't exactly a thing back then, unfortunately.

When Skating Sensations of 1950 travelled west to Vancouver and New Westminster, British Columbia, throngs of show-goers had to be turned away at the gate because there simply wasn't enough seating. At three shows in the Maritimes, there were so many attendees that extra chairs had to be placed directly on the ice.

It's really hard to put into words just how big of a deal Barbara Ann was at this point, but the first-hand writings of those who attended the show in newspapers, yearbooks and diaries help to give a sense of her celebrity. When the tour stopped in Sarnia, Ontario, a crowd of looky-loos gathered on the street just to peer in the glass window of her hotel's dining room and watch her eat. In St. Andrews-by-the-Sea, New Brunswick, all nine hundred of the summer resort town's winter residents showed up to watch at least one of the three shows. In Saint John, children were let out of school so they could wave at Barbara Ann when she got off the train. In Kamloops, British Columbia, she was given a baby seal jacket and a ten-gallon hat and proclaimed "Queen of Cow Country". In Kelowna, she was given a brooch with a key and a citation that read, "This is an emblem of the fact that having already won the keys of our hearts, we now offer you the keys of our city."

Residents of Prince Edward Island - the land of *Anne with an E* - showed up in droves to see Barbara Ann (without an E) perform at the Charlottetown Forum, which almost didn't happen because the ferry over to the Island was stuck in the ice for six hours. Though skaters like Fanny and John Davidson and Cecil Smith and Melville Rogers had wowed Islanders with exhibitions decades prior, Skating Sensations of 1950 was the first full-scale tour to visit the Island. The Lieutenant Governor, Premier and Mayor of Charlottetown all attended the show and lavished Barbara Ann with gifts, including a gold locket and an oil painting. Philanthropist Wanda Lefurgey Wyatt bought her tickets a month in advance and spent almost three dollars - no paltry sum in those days - for the return bus trip from Summerside to Charlottetown. "Show was lovely," she wrote in her diary. "B. Anne charming."

While Skating Sensations of 1950 was making headlines,

Melville Rogers remarked, "People forget that Babs was never an American heroine whereas every home in Canada has [a] well-rounded knowledge of their favourite. She was only a printed name to most New Yorkers in her debut there. Again, she appeared in a movie house. However, she is now doing exactly what Sonja Henie had to do before she got intimately known - and that is barnstorming across the country... She has really learned, on this tour, how to inject showmanship into the classical skating she performs better than any girl on Earth."

The tour wasn't all sunshine and rainbows though. Less than a month into the tour, word was received that the Minto Skating Club's rink, where Barbara Ann had trained her entire career, had burned to the ground in a devastating fire. On the way to a show in Valleyfield, Quebec, the tour's bus got caught in the snow. Members of the cast had to be transported the rest of the way on an open sleigh. In Barrie, the Mayor refused to have anything to do with a 'civic reception' planned in conjunction with the tour, claiming that such a reception would have been appropriate if she was touring the country for charity - not for personal gain. Tommy Gorman received a letter one day from a disgruntled show-goer who said: "All we needed was a strip-tease act to make the show complete." The lights failed during the *Showboat* number in Kitchener-Waterloo, stranding Barbara Ann and Jerry Rehfield on a makeshift bridge. Barbara Ann remembered, "We stood there smiling... waiting for the lights to go on. When they didn't, we had to find our way out in the darkness."

In Vernon, British Columbia, Barbara Ann skated with a temperature of one hundred and two. At the Calgary show, she started having serious pain in her side. A doctor examined her and determined she had a broken rib, a bad cold and pleurisy. He ordered two weeks of bed rest. She told the doctor that she simply couldn't cancel the shows, and his compromise was that if she continued to skate with a plaster over her rib, she had to cancel all personal appearances and rest between shows.

Barbara Ann's injury and illness forced her to cancel a public appearance at the Hudson's Bay store in Edmonton, where she was to have autographed children's Barbara Ann Scott dolls. The *Edmonton Journal* ran a picture of disappointed children waiting at the store, next to pictures of Barbara Ann resting in her bathrobe at the hotel. Local newspaper reporters and radio announcers grabbed ahold of the story and ran with it, framing Barbara Ann as a prima donna with "bad manners" and inventing a feud between Tommy Gorman and Mary. In reality, Tommy Gorman called Mary the "real heroine of the trip." She acted as a surrogate mother and nurse to the entire cast and tried to keep Barbara Ann in good spirits when the press turned on her.

"I was terribly upset," Barbara Ann recalled. "When I went out of the hotel and walked down the street, I felt like a criminal. At a press conference, you could have cut the atmosphere with a knife. But after I had explained the true facts of the matter, several radio stations interviewed me to give me a chance to explain in public." Tommy Gorman turned the PR disaster into a triumph by staging a free show for children under the age of ten, which was attended by over ten thousand children. "Everybody in the company expected to see no audience but perhaps some flying eggs and tomatoes," remembered Barbara Ann. "The place was packed. I was grateful to the people for being so understanding and the crowd was just about the most enthusiastic of the entire tour."

The tour made two stops south of the border in New York state, then did its rounds in the Maritimes before looping back to Quebec for the final performances in April of 1950.

13

"I wanted to win the Olympics. Even as a little girl, that was my ultimate goal. By and by, it got to be automatic. I just kept going. Suddenly I realized I'd done it, and could stop." - Barbara Ann Scott

On May 4, 1950, Barbara Ann was the special guest star at the premiere of the Ice Capades in Hollywood. She was a huge hit in Tinseltown and was the only performer in the show called on for encores. After the show, she posed for pictures with Nancy Davis, Gary Steffen, Jane Powell and a young Hollywood star who would later serve as the 40th President of the United States, Ronald Reagan.

After the show, Barbara Ann took a month's vacation at the Algonquin Resort in St. Andrews by-the-Sea, New Brunswick and laid the cornerstone of the new hockey stadium in St. John's, Newfoundland. Canada's newest province was the only one she was unable to visit on the Skating Sensations of 1950 tour. The province's first Premier, Joey Smallwood, gifted her a fur coat.

For six weeks in the summer of 1950, Barbara Ann starred in Rose Marie on Ice at the Harringay Arena in London, England with Michael Kirby, Pat Gregory and Heinie Brock. Billed as the "first full-length musical ever to be presented on ice", the show was a traditional British pantomime, where a narrator read the plot over loudspeakers, accompanied by music, and the cast mimed out the dialogue. A precision number with thirty-six men dressed as Mounties was a highlight of the Canadian-themed show.

After the run of Rose Marie on Ice ended, Barbara Ann returned to Canada. She and Mary moved from Ottawa to an apartment on Avenue Road in North Toronto, so she could take advantage of her life membership and skate at the Granite Club, where Mr. Galbraith was coaching at the time. Plans for a Skating Sensations of 1951 tour the following year fell through because Barbara Ann had committed to return to England for another run of Rose Marie on Ice the following year. Tommy Gorman tried to get triple-threat skater/actress/dancer Belita Jepson-Turner to replace Barbara Ann but Belita's contract with Monogram didn't allow it. Like Barbara Ann, Belita went to England, where she starred in Babes of the Wood on Ice and London Melody at Empress Hall.

Barbara Ann enjoyed the brief break from skating immensely. She cooked, sewed, sketched and read mystery stories. "Except for a few short holidays, I can't remember ever having had time to loaf," she told a reporter. "That's why I'm enjoying this winter with no shows to do. It's a holiday for my mother too, who works as hard at my career as I do... if we are not tossed out because of the dogs we'll at least have time to bake cakes and make muffins for tea and have friends in to eat them."

In early 1951, Barbara Ann starred in the Minto Follies, the Skating Club of Boston's Ice Chips show and the Vancouver Skating Club's carnival, before returning to England for the revival of Rose Marie on Ice. Her salary for this show, paid directly to the Foundation, was twenty-five hundred pounds a week.

Newspaper reporters had been faithfully reporting that Barbara Ann was fighting off movie producers since she had turned professional, but nothing ever came of it. *Flash* magazine claimed that "the reason - never given out publicly - was a weak voice and not-so-photogenic face. And that was that."

Barbara Ann never had any real interest in being a big movie star like Sonja Henie. "I was never screen-struck," she said. "I never bought movie magazines, never clipped pictures of screen stars. I've gone into the bedrooms of my girlfriends and found the walls covered with 'millions' of pictures of movie stars but I never wanted to do the same."

The press wasn't only fixated on Barbara Ann's potential as a Hollywood star. They were obsessed with comparing her with Sonja Henie.

Whenever reporters grilled Barbara Ann about Sonja, there was always an awkward silence and a firm but polite response: "I admire her very much. I've always admired her." Reporters were hell-bent on inventing a feud. During one interview, Barbara Ann lost her cool and scolded her interviewer: "I wish you would not compare me with Miss Henie. That is not fair to either one of us. We are different types. Her skating was vivacious, peppy." It didn't help that Melville Rogers and Donald B. Cruikshank, two very influential men in her orbit, were the first to fan the flames by telling reporters that Barbara Ann was a better skater than Sonja. The rivalry was fuelled by both star's publicity agents. *Time* magazine published an article pitting the two stars against each other, which was very uncomplimentary of Sonja. In reality, the two had a lot in common – they both won the Olympics and World Championships. They had parents who were very supportive of their skating and they had a lot of dedication and drive.

While Barbara Ann was in England performing with Rose Marie on Ice, Sonja had a huge falling out with Arthur M. Wirtz, who produced the Hollywood Ice Revue tour she starred in. Barbara Ann received a call from her agents offering her the starring role. Along with top billing came a salary of over one hundred thousand dollars a year.

Sonja didn't take the news well. In an interview with an Ottawa reporter, she announced she wanted to "skate against Barbara Ann in her hometown" for a twenty thousand dollar prize for the title of World's Professional Champion. Sonja suggested that both she and Barbara Ann put up ten thousand dollars for a winner-take-all prize and said, "There simply is not room for two World's Champions in our business, and this is as good a time as any to decide who is tops." Barbara Ann said she would be happy to do it, but the competition never happened. If either of them had been serious about it, they could have competed at the long-established World Professional Championships in England.

Aside from a brief stint performing in Tom Arnold's ice pantomime Robinson Crusoe on Ice in Zürich, Switzerland in October, Barbara Ann spent most of the fall of 1951 in rehearsals for the Hollywood Ice Revue.

The tour opened to high praise in Milwaukee, Wisconsin on November 7, 1951, with eight thousand people attending the first show. While Barbara Ann was in Indianapolis performing at the Coliseum, Sonja was skating at the Cow Palace in Daly City, California with a cast of loyal skaters she had poached from the Hollywood Ice Revue, in her own tour called the Sonja Henie Ice Revue.

The Hollywood Ice Revue was selling tickets by the fistful, and the Sonja Henie Ice Revue was struggling financially. Arthur M. Wirtz bailed Sonja out with a hundred thousand dollar cheque, no strings attached.

Nine thousand people came out to see Barbara Ann skate on Christmas Day in Chicago. On January 17, 1952, the tour opened at Madison Square Garden in New York City. Over sixty-eight thousand people attended the show over a three-day period, which was a new attendance record for any ice show in New York City. During her time with the Hollywood Ice Revue, Barbara Ann appeared on popular television programs like *The Ken Murray Show* and *What's My Line?* Over the years, she also did commercials for everything from Avon cosmetics, Timex watches and Community silverware to Canada Dry ginger ale, Florida oranges and Sunkist frozen lemonade. She even threw the first ball at a Toronto Blue Jays game, while her poodle Pierre ran around the bases.

Barbara Ann made a special trip to British Columbia in March to star in the Vancouver Skating Club's carnival, as a special favour to her former coach Mr. Gold. Rumours of a feud between her and Andra McLaughlin, who had the dressing room next to her when they toured together in the Hollywood Ice Revue, took off like a house on fire. Andra's mother was very upset that Barbara Ann came to do the show because Andra was supposed to have been billed as the star. Barbara Ann didn't even know Andra very well, and some felt that the whole thing was a publicity stunt conjured up by the Vancouver Skating Club to sell tickets.

In April, the tour came north to Toronto for a week-long stint at Maple Leaf Gardens. Barbara Ann was particularly appreciative of the boisterous Canadian audience, remarking, "In New York, the audiences aren't too responsive. They seem to sit there and say 'Entertain me'. But the people here appreciate and understand skating. They're wonderful."

The night that the show opened, Barbara Ann's Toronto apartment was ransacked by thieves, who stole thousands of dollars of jewelry and furs. Two months later, a box was found under some evergreen trees by a milk truck driver, containing an empty wallet, an empty watch-box, a Granite Club membership card and several of Barbara Ann's personal papers.

When the Hollywood Ice Revue wrapped up for the season, Barbara Ann appeared on tank ice at the Conrad Hilton Hotel in Chicago before vacationing at the Tower Isle Hotel in Jamaica. Rehearsals for the next season's Hollywood Ice Revue kicked off in August.

Barbara Ann was delighted to hear that Andrea Kékesy Bernolák, the 1949 World Champion in pairs skating, had defected from Hungary to Canada and joined the Minto Skating Club. Andrea told reporters, "I longed to come to this country... I met Barbara Ann at the Olympic Games at St. Moritz and she told me of the freedom you Canadians enjoy here. And, too, she told me of the skating here. I could not be happy until I came."

By this point, Barbara Ann was already starting to become disillusioned with touring. She was a homebody at heart and didn't enjoy living out of trunks. She brought pots and pans on the road with her and requested hotel rooms with kitchenettes so that she could cook, but never felt at home in hotels. She also felt like an outcast at times, because she didn't smoke or drink. "I didn't like it, period," she later said. "I think people in show business tend to become very artificial and live in their own little world. I was the star, and some of them didn't know whether they should talk to me or not. I was never more lonely in my life. The public thinks that the star of an ice show lies in bed all day, and just appears for a couple of hours in the evening, makes pots of money and saves it all, and has lines of eligible bachelors waiting at the stage door. It just isn't true. You rehearse for hours. You have to wear awful false eyelashes and make-up half an inch thick. There are taxes to pay, and people who work for you. You don't see your friends because they hesitate to bother you, and the people who do come backstage are mostly tiresome types - anxious to tell their friends that they were there. I must admit that as a show skater, I was less than sensational. I wasn't the muscular type who [could] leap three feet in the air. Everything I did looked too easy. Actually, I did some quite difficult things. I'd do a double loop jump, and maybe one person in the audience would clap. The audience preferred something more dramatic, like spins. Most of all, I hated it when they made me do a wriggle. I felt like an idiot."

The tour would often reuse numbers and draw their themes from well-known films and books. One year she was Goldilocks again; the next Gretel in *Hansel and Gretel*. One number she did quite enjoy was a retelling of *The Wizard of Oz*. During her number to "Over The Rainbow", Pierre, who was playing Toto, would crawl around the ice following her. At one show, people were in hysterics when he lifted his leg to pee. Sadly, Pierre died at a veterinary hospital in Chicago. She got another poodle called Mon Homme, to take his place.

After five years of touring, Barbara Ann

unceremoniously skated her final performance with the Hollywood Ice Revue in Cincinnati, Ohio on March 13, 1955. Arthur M. Wirtz had given Tommy Gorman a leave of absence to organize a final Canadian tour starring Barbara Ann, but she decided to call it quits. She had met the man of her dreams.

14

"You know how most people get depressed if they wake up in the morning and it's raining? Barb looks out the window and says, 'Never mind, it will probably clear by noon'... Think what a wonderful world it would be if we were all like that." - Tommy King

Barbara Ann was not a fan of Tommy King at first. When she was in London skating in Rose Marie on Ice and the offer had come to tour with the Hollywood Ice Revue, she had read a quote in the paper from Tommy, who was Arthur M. Wirtz's publicity agent, saying that he had "not yet decided how he was going to glamourize Miss Scott." She was so annoyed by the quote that she threatened to get off the plane when she came home with her hair down and wearing bobby socks, but Mary talked her out of it.

"I immediately said to myself, there's a man I'm not going to like," recalled Barbara Ann. "I pictured him as middle-aged and pudgy, wearing a baggy suit and smoking a cigar. That was my idea of a publicity man. Instead, he turned out to be young and baby-faced and quite the nicest person I had ever known."

Barbara Ann and Tommy, who was a former professional basketball player with the Detroit Falcons, were good friends for several years before they got engaged. They were married at the Rosedale

Presbyterian Church in Toronto on September 17, 1955. She wore a long-sleeved white French silk brocade dress with a train. Every seat at the small church was filled, and more than four hundred fans and well-wishers gathered outside to catch a glimpse of The Queen of The Ice on her wedding day. At the reception at the Roof Garden of the Royal York Hotel, the couple danced on a miniature skating rink. It was a royal skating wedding. Her matron of honour was her old friend Margaret (McGuinness) Burka, who had accompanied her to the 1948 Winter Olympics. Canadian Pairs Champion Donald Gilchrist's wife was one of her attendants. Her coaches Mr. Gold and Mr. Galbraith were in attendance and a telegram of congratulations from Dick Button was read at the reception.

After honeymooning in Mexico, Barbara Ann and Tommy settled in Chicago. The couple lived in a five-room apartment on the fourteenth floor of a grey-stone building on East Pearson Street, in Chicago's north side, near Lake Michigan. Tommy worked as the Vice-President in charge of advertising and public relations at Merchandise Mart. They had a turtle named Bertyl, a budgie named Leroy and a poodle named Prince. They had a subscription to the Book of the Month Club and enjoyed playing golf, taking dance lessons and swimming in the pool in the basement of their building together. Barbara Ann expressed an interest in Christian Science. Her competitive side came out whenever they played parlour games. Like a true Taurus, she was always determined to win. The couple never had children of their own, though Barbara Ann was the stepmother of

Tommy's children from a previous marriage, who lived with their mother.

A perfectionist at heart, Barbara Ann loved to knit, but when she made even the smallest mistake, she would rip back row after row of stitches to correct it. This obsession with perfection and order carried over into her home life. In an interview with Dorothy Sangster, Barbara Ann said, "You've probably heard I have this thing about tidiness. I like a clean house and everything in order. I dust my window ledges every morning, take the shades off the lamps, straighten out things in the medicine cabinet... and take all the books out of the bookshelves so I can dust them properly. I think anyone who's a good housekeeper does the same as I do, but a lot of my friends seem to think it's very funny. They did kid me because I give Tommy his breakfast in bed on a tray, lay out his tie and socks, and shine his razor, but a husband has to work all day and I think he should be comfortable at home. Besides, if you aren't going to devote yourself to your husband, why marry?" Barbara Ann's views on marriage were seen as very old-fashioned, even in the 1950s. Angela Burke, writing a feature on her for the *Star Weekly*, surmised her views as "treason to feminists".

Aside from some commercial work, Barbara Ann's final skating performance was an NBC television special on New Year's Day, 1956. In the production, hosted by Art Linkletter, Barbara Ann skated an ice ballet choreographed by John Butler with Dick Button. Legendary torch singer Peggy Lee also appeared in the special. Her last time on skates was in the late 1960s when she appeared in a Maxwell House coffee commercial filmed at Rockefeller Center in New York.

Barbara Ann kept her palladium skates, skating trophies and a framed collection of gold medals and awards on display in an upstairs study. "Tommy likes me to keep them out where they can be seen. He's very proud of them. I'd just as soon pack them away," she said. "They belong to another time in my life that's over and done with. Today I'm Tommy's wife and I have the future to think of."

In 1956, Barbara Ann was recruited to serve as a hostess at several Democratic Party events. She began working with the Democrats during that year's National Convention in Chicago and was an ardent supporter of future President John F. Kennedy, who narrowly lost his bid to become the Party's candidate for Vice-President that year. Senator Kennedy's father owned the Merchandise Mart where Tommy worked. Though Barbara Ann couldn't vote because she wasn't an American citizen, she expressed a desire to "work for the Democrats in any way she possibly can." She was an enthusiastic supporter of John F. Kennedy for many years and was involved in the Sportsmen for Kennedy campaign during the 1960 Presidential Election. In addition to her political work, Barbara Ann was also a member of two animal charities: the Humane Society and the Anti-Vivesectionist League.

Barbara Ann tried her hand at being a director in 1957

when she was put in charge of the summer season at the Edgewater Beach Playhouse. She directed five productions over eleven weeks, which starred acting greats like Burgess Meredith, Ann Sheridan and Melvyn Douglas. She was more comfortable in the kitchen than the director's seat, and one of her favourite desserts to make, when she entertained, was her Moist Banana Cake:

Start heating oven to 350°. Then sift together:

2 cups sifted cake flour
1 tsp. baking soda
1/4 tsp. salt

With fork, mash thoroughly:

4 or 5 ripe bananas (1 1/2 cups mashed)

Then, with spoon, cream together thoroughly:

1/2 cup soft butter or margarine
1 1/2 cups granulated sugar

Now add and beat until fluffy and creamy:

2 eggs

Then beat in thoroughly mashed bananas and:

1 tsp. vanilla extract

Add flour mixture alternately with:

1/2 cup buttermilk

Beat after each addition until just mixed. Turn mixture into 8 X 8 X 2 baking pan lined on bottom with waxed paper. Bake cake 1 1/4 hours, or until done. After cake cools about 10 min., turn it out of pan. When cake is completely cool, frost top with vanilla butter frosting, and garnish with sliced bananas. (Or frost cake with whipped cream, and garnish with grated unsweetened chocolate.)

One of Barbara Ann's most interesting post-skating projects was her stint as the owner of the Barbara Ann Scott Beauty Salon. The salon opened in June of 1959 on Tudor Court in Glencoe, a well-to-do Chicago suburb. The salon had a giant picture of Barbara Ann in a skating pose on the white brick wall facing the entrance and a maid who went around with a coffee cart while people were getting their hair done. Barbara Ann left the management of the business, which lasted just over ten years, up to Philip Penzo, her hairstylist when she was touring with the Hollywood Ice Revue. Before opening the salon, Barbara Ann and Tommy had toyed around with the idea of opening a skating school instead but decided against it.

Barbara Ann's childhood dream of owning a horse came true when Tommy bought a pair of riding horses, Princess Pearlie May and King's Regal Tipper. She spent four hours a day riding and tending to the horses at the stables at Morton Grove and particularly enjoyed schooling horses in equitation. Over a nearly forty-year period, she won more than four hundred first-place ribbons in country horse shows with Regal Tipper, who was Tommy's horse. While Tommy played golf in the summers, she would load Princess Pearl and King's Regal Tipper into a trailer, hitch it up to her car and drive them to shows in small little towns in Michigan, Indiana, Wisconsin and Illinois. She enjoyed horseback riding competitions immensely. "I like it much better with horses than with skating," she once said. "On skates, you're out there all by yourself. When a person wins in equitation... [they] usually put their own name on the trophy, but I always put the horse's name on because he's the true athlete."

On November 22, 1963, President Kennedy was assassinated in Dallas, Texas. Barbara Ann was in Toronto at the time making a special appearance at the Canadian Figure Skating Association's Olympic Trials at Maple Leaf Gardens. Debbi Wilkes recalled, "There was a very great pall that came over the crowd. I remember her being quite moved and she was kind of operating on autopilot. You could tell that she was quite shaken. At the time, as a teenager, I didn't fully comprehend the seriousness of her reaction. It must have been very difficult for her to carry out her responsibilities, but she was thoroughly lovely... It was the first time I ever met her, and of course I was totally starstruck. She was very generous in her comments. She had very obviously studied us all, which of course made us all feel very important - that Barbara Ann would have, in some measure, followed our careers. We were all very flattered by her attention. She was extremely gracious."

Barbara Ann lost several other people that she cared about in the 1960s and 70s. In February of 1961, U.S. coach Maribel Vinson Owen, who had been a big supporter of her skating in her journalism days, tragically passed away in the Sabena crash in Belgium that killed the entire American figure skating team. Two months later, Tommy Gorman, the organizer of her Skating Sensations of 1950 tour passed away.

In 1965, the body of Barbara Ann's old friendly rival Gretchen Van Zandt Merrill was found in the living room of her Windsor, Connecticut apartment, near a case filled with her skating trophies. She had been dead for four days when she was found. Though her cause of death was never revealed publicly, Barbara Ann's one-time choreographer Osborne Colson said that she committed suicide.

In 1977, Barbara Ann's beloved coach Mr. Gold suffered serious injuries in a horrific fire in his apartment in Scarborough. He fell asleep while smoking in bed and his mattress caught on fire. He carried the burning mattress to the bathroom to try to dowse the flames, but it caught fire to the curtains and a cupboard. He was overcome by the smoke and suffered from carbon monoxide poisoning and third-degree burns to the lower part of his body. He died in the hospital the next day.

After Mr. Gold's death, Barbara Ann was inducted into the World Figure Skating Hall of Fame and named

Chancellor of a new post-secondary institute for fashion design and fashion merchandising in Toronto - the International Academy of Merchandising and Design Canada. The original school was located in Tommy's Merchandise Mart and by the 1990s, there were two more campuses in Montreal and Tampa.

In December of 1986, Mary passed away at the age of ninety-four. She had lived out her golden years in an apartment in Toronto. Every afternoon, she and several well-to-do friends, all of them fellow widows, would go to the Granite Club for dinner. Ever-present by Barbara Ann's side throughout her skating career, Mary unfairly earned a nickname – the Dowager Queen. Some people assumed that she was something of a stage mother because she would often take the lead whenever the press asked Barbara Ann questions.

Mary described herself as "polite but firm" and she had a reputation for being blunt and very outspoken, but always putting Barbara Ann's best interests first. Mary said, "It's Barbara Ann's show. I just go along for the ride... You have to have a lot of patience and be willing to devote a great deal of time to your child. Every child is better for attention, but having a child who is following a career means giving up a lot of social life. But I liked doing it... Barbara Ann was asked to speak to a group of schoolchildren and give them advice on achieving their goals in life. And her words were: 'You have to have a real determination, and the courage to stick to it.' I think those words from my little girl demonstrate how I have tried to bring her up... If I had any guiding principle, it would be that I was going to bring my child up *myself*. And it wasn't always easy." Barbara Ann pushed back against the rumours that her mother had forced her to do something she didn't want to do. "I know she's been accused of being the big bad bear that made me skate, but it's not true," she said. "Lots of times she urged me to come off the ice and have fun with the other children. I was the one who wanted to skate. I was determined to win the Olympics for Canada."

In November of 1987, Barbara Ann was invited to be one of the first two torch bearers in the Olympic Torch Relay before the 1988 Winter Olympic Games in Calgary. It was a top-secret affair. She came to St. John's, Newfoundland incognito in a black wig and glasses, under the pseudonym Bonnie Grace.

Barbara Ann and race walker Ferd Hayward walked the first of the eighteen thousand kilometers in the Torch Relay in Signal Hill. It was a thrilling moment. "To an athlete, the Olympic torch is almost sacred," Barbara Ann said. "To be this close to it, to have the honour of carrying it with Ferd... I can't find words." Tragically, Ferd drowned in a pond near St. John's less than a year later.

Barbara Ann was also one of many Canadian skating legends who appeared in a star-studded figure skating performance in the Closing Ceremony of the Calgary Games. Elizabeth Manley met Barbara Ann for the first time at those Games. She recalled, "I had a private meeting the afternoon before the night I won and that was such an inspiration. It was such a motivation. I just remember her hugging and kissing me like she'd known me my whole life and she knew so much about me which impressed me so much... You just don't think someone like that would... From the moment she walked in, she just made me feel at ease and she inspired me and gave me great encouragement and motivation... I got to meet my hero." Forty years after Barbara Ann won Olympic gold in St. Moritz, Elizabeth Manley won the free skate and silver medal in Calgary. Barbara Ann and Elizabeth shared both a friendship and a nickname - "Canada's Sweetheart".

15

"She was a character. She was a pistol. She didn't hesitate to voice her opinion. She always did it beautifully, but she was certainly no shrinking violet." - Debbi Wilkes

After the Calgary Olympics, Barbara Ann started to become more involved in the sport again. She was a perennial judge and referee at professional figure skating competitions and was invited by the Canadian Figure Skating Association to act as a guest of honour for many years at the Canadian Figure Skating Championships. With Tommy by her side, she tirelessly signed autographs for long line-ups of adoring fans and presented awards to the winners. Though she had lived in the United States for many years, Canada was still home and she never gave up her citizenship.

Debbi Wilkes vividly remembered a chance encounter with Barbara Ann in 1994, when the Canadian Figure Skating Championships were in Edmonton: "I was working doing the broadcast. We were staying in the same hotel, but of course, she was managed like a Hollywood superstar. I had to get myself to the venue however I could. I'm standing outside of the hotel - I don't know if I was waiting for somebody or waiting for a cab - and all of a sudden, this big limo pulls up in front of me and Barb puts the window down and goes, 'Debbi! I'm going to the same place you are! Hop in!' She was in her shoes and mink and jewels. I made a comment about her attire and she said, 'Oh, this is just a costume!' The crowd knew who she was and she played her role very, very well but in my mind, didn't take it too seriously. She was very human, very self-deprecating and saw the humour in everything and yet, appreciated how she could add to the lustre of the event. My impression was that she did not take herself very seriously but wanted to use her stardom for the benefit of the sport. It was an interesting lesson for me, and I really appreciated the role model she played."

Barbara Ann was always dressed to the nines, whether it be in a ball gown or one of her many matching Gino Rossi Ultrasuede suits when she made public appearances. She owned over a hundred hats and had an impressive collection of emeralds and diamonds. She cared about skin care and wore Estée Lauder and Revlon cosmetics and fake eyelashes. The same Chicago hairdresser, Madame Calli at the Salon de Paris, coloured her hair for over thirty years. "I'm not fussing with pageboys or fancy up-dos," she said. "I'd look like an old hag if I wore my hair in a pageboy."

Barbara Ann was also a proud client of Chicago plastic surgeon Dr. Annette Hoffman. "I go to a cosmetic surgeon and I don't make any bones about it," she admitted. "I think it's so silly when people look marvellous and they say 'I didn't do a thing.'... If your dress was baggy, you would take it in. If your face bags, you take it in. I have a handsome husband, and I don't want him looking at other women." She took great pride in her appearance. "I never think about my age," she admitted. "It's how I feel that counts. Show business taught me to look presentable on all occasions. I never even wanted to see the garbage man if my makeup wasn't perfect."

In 1991, Barbara Ann was inducted into the Canadian Figure Skating Association's Hall of Fame and invested as an Officer of the Order of Canada. The following year, she fell on a Chicago sidewalk right before Christmas, seriously injured her knee and fractured her leg in three places. The doctors told her she would never have full use of her knee again. After multiple surgeries and months of physiotherapy, she proved them wrong and was able to make a guest appearance at the IBM Skates of Gold show in 1993 alongside fellow Olympic Gold Medallists in women's figure skating Kristi Yamaguchi, Katarina Witt, Anett Pötzsch, Peggy Fleming, Trixi Schuba, Tenley Albright and Jeannette Altwegg.

Like everyone, Barbara Ann was shocked when Nancy Kerrigan was violently attacked in 1994, in the lead-up to the Winter Olympic Games in Lillehammer. Reflecting on her own experience with the "47-U1" convertible in 1947, she said that there was no way that Tonya Harding would have been allowed to go to the Olympics back in her day. "Avery Brundage is probably turning in his grave," she said. "If he'd had so much as a whiff of a scandal surrounding any Olympic athletes they'd be disqualified immediately... Harming a human being is beyond understanding."

In 1996, Barbara Ann helped officially open the World Figure Skating Championships at City Hall in Edmonton. Hundreds showed up and gave her a standing ovation. While in Edmonton, she made a special visit to the Mewburn Veterans Centre. Visiting veterans was something she often made a point of doing during her competitive career, and she felt both a duty and desire to do it. "My father was a First World War veteran and my husband was a marine, so we're from a military background," she told the veterans she visited. "When I was a little girl learning to compete, many of you sent good-luck charms and telegrams, and that's what helped me do what I did for Canada, and I thank you with all of my heart."

Barbara Ann and Tommy moved to a house on the beach on Amelia Island, off Florida's Atlantic Coast, in 1997. Retired life suited them well, and they embraced their lives as "permanent Snowbirds."

1998 was a banner year for Barbara Ann, but it wasn't an easy one. She had agreed to make a dizzying series of public appearances in conjunction with the fiftieth anniversary of her Olympic gold medal win, but she wasn't in great health at the time. She spent a week in the hospital, with viral pneumonia in both lungs, before flying to Hamilton to serve as the Honorary Chair of the Canadian Figure Skating Championships. In June, she was honoured as one of the first inductees in Canada's Walk of Fame, alongside legendary musicians and authors like Anne Murray, Gordon Lightfoot and Pierre Berton. She spent Canada Day in Ottawa, at a seniors brunch at the Aberdeen Pavilion in Landsdowne Park. The brunch was a special occasion indeed, as she was reunited with surviving members of the RCAF Flyers hockey team from the 1948 Winter Olympics. CBC's *Life & Times* also re-aired *Queen of the Blades*, a one-hour documentary on Barbara Ann's story, which was first released in 1997.

Behind closed doors, Barbara Ann had a great sense of humour and was never afraid to speak her mind about the changes in the figure skating world in the decades since she retired. She was a vocal and eloquent supporter of the compulsory figures and thought the decision to remove them from international competition was idiotic. If they weren't television-friendly, she figured, they didn't need to be shown on broadcasts. She thought it was great that the line between amateurism and professional skating became more blurred, and skaters were able to make money during their amateur careers to support themselves. She was a big fan of both Kurt Browning and Elvis Stojko and thought the technical advancements in the sport in the 1990s were incredible, but that the number of triple jumps skaters had to include in their programs to be competitive was extremely excessive, as they were just acrobatics. She thought the IJS system of judging made programs too formulaic. She felt that programs were more beautiful to watch under the 6.0 system. The choreography was more individual and the footwork suited the music and was less mechanical-looking. The free skate, in her estimation, was meant to be a free skate, not another short program with required elements. When Dick

Button formed the World Skating Federation in protest of the International Skating Union after the judging scandal at the 2002 Winter Olympics, she was an ardent supporter. She knew what she liked and what she didn't when it came to figure skating, but was supportive of progress – if it was progress. Choreographer Sandra Bezic aptly noted, "Barbara Ann hasn't closed her mind to the changes in skating. She doesn't just write things off because they didn't happen in her day."

What many people may not realize is that Barbara Ann and Tommy quietly donated over a hundred thousand dollars to promising young Ottawa figure skaters through scholarships administered through a trust set up with the Minto Skating Club. Giving back was something she believed strongly in. Debbi Wilkes recalled, "I complimented her once... and she said something like, 'Skating has given me my life. I owe it something back.' It was very touching how she had a real perspective on the sport, her contribution to it and its contribution to her life."

Barbara Ann continued to make many trips to Canada in the years that followed, appearing in the Legendary Night of Figure Skating at Air Canada Centre in 1999 and as a guest of honour at the Minto Skating Club's centenary. At the reception at the Chateau Laurier, "O Canada" played and Barbara Ann opened her speech with "Minto is my club, Ottawa is my home, and Canada is my country". At the Canadian Tulip Festival in 2004, she became the first person to be given the key to the City of Ottawa twice. In 2006, Skate Canada renamed its new Headquarters the Barbara Ann Scott Building. Barbara Ann was wheeled out onto the ice in a red Mustang convertible for a ceremony at that year's Canadian Figure Skating Championships.

In 2008, Barbara Ann was invited to be a special guest of honour at the Ottawa Viennese Winter Ball, along with Liz Manley, Debbi Wilkes and Frances Dafoe. When a photographer approached her for a picture alone, she answered, "Absolutely not. All of the medallists will be in this picture." She got her way and Liz, Debbi and Frances were included in the picture. "She wasn't just looking for her own power, she was always looking out for everybody else's too," remembered Debbi Wilkes.

Two months later, Barbara Ann went out for dinner with friends in Jacksonville to celebrate her eightieth birthday. She delighted in any occasion spent with Tommy. She joked, "We call ourselves the little old couple. We shuffle around and have a good time." Tommy financed the building of the Holy Trinity Anglican Church in Fernandina Beach and played drums in a classical jazz band, Tom King and the Royal Chicagoans. Kurt Browning called Barbara Ann and Tommy Grandma and Grandpa.

In December of 2009, eighty-one-year-old Barbara Ann was invited to carry the Olympic torch into the House of Commons to the Speaker's chair, as part of the Olympic Torch Relay before the 2010 Winter Olympics. Beforehand, she ran around Fernandina Beach with her heavy garden shears over her head to practice carrying something of that weight. She later had the great privilege of carrying the Olympic flag in the Vancouver Games, along with Anne Murray, Bobby Orr, Jacques Villeneuve, Julie Payette, Donald Sutherland, Senator Romeo Dallaire and Terry Fox's mother Betty.

Barbara Ann made her final visit to Canada in August of 2012, to open a gallery at City Hall that showed off over three hundred artifacts from her skating career she donated to the City of Ottawa Archives. Barbara Ann was in considerable pain after surgery for pancreatic and abdominal problems that March, but was radiant and beautifully spoken during what turned out to be her final public speech.

The trip took its toll and Barbara Ann passed away peacefully at her home in Fernandina Beach, with Tommy by her side, on September 30, 2012. She was eighty-four years old. It was like the Queen had died. Tributes poured in from figure skating legends like Dick Button, Kurt Browning, Donald Jackson, Elizabeth Manley, Frances Dafoe and Joannie Rochette. Her death made the national evening news across Canada and Ottawa's City Hall flew all of their flags at half-mast in tribute to her.

Barbara Ann inspired thousands of Canadians to work hard, follow their dreams and strive for excellence. She was a true champion both on and off the ice. She will always be remembered as our Queen of the Ice.

APPENDIX A - FIRSTS

First Canadian woman to land a double Lutz jump in competition (1942)

First woman and first figure skater to win the Lou E. Marsh Memorial Trophy (1945) and the first athlete in any sport to be awarded the trophy three times (1945, 1947, 1948)

First figure skater to win the Velma Springstead Trophy for Canada's top female athlete twice (1945, 1947)

First person to win the Women's Amateur Athletic Federation of Canada's Bobbie Rosenfeld Award for Most Outstanding Woman Athlete three times in a row (1946, 1947, 1948)

First Canadian skater to both compete in and win a gold medal at European Championships (1947, 1948)

First and only Canadian skater to hold the European and North American title at the same time (1947)

First champion of any sport to have been formally congratulated by both the Governments of Canada and Ontario (1947)

First Canadian skater to win a gold medal at Winter Olympic Games (1948)

First Canadian woman to win a gold medal at the World Figure Skating Championships (1948)

First woman in history to receive University College's Literary & Athletic Society's colours (1948)

First person to receive a Pathfinder's Badge without earning it through war service (1948)

First woman to be named an honorary member of the Toronto Press Club (1948)

First Canadian figure skater to be featured on the cover of "Time" magazine (1948)

First freewoman of the City of Ottawa (1948)

First figure skater to be inducted into the Canadian Olympic Hall of Fame (1949)

First figure skater to be inducted into Ottawa's Sports Hall of Fame (1966)

First figure skater to be inducted into Canada's Walk of Fame (1998)

APPENDIX B - COMPETITIVE RECORD

1937 Minto Skating Club Competition for Girls Under 12 (Devonshire Cup) - 1st
1938 Minto Skating Club Reynolds' Prize (Girls) - 2nd
1938 Minto Skating Club Potsdam Shield (3rd Class Skaters) - 2nd
1938 Minto Skating Club Gilmore Memorial (Intermediate Girls) - 1st
1938 Minto Skating Club Competition for Girls Under 12 (Devonshire Cup) - 1st
1939 Canadian Figure Skating Championships - 5th (junior)
1939 Lake Placid Annual Open Summer Competition - 1st (senior)
1939 Lake Placid Annual Open Summer Competition - 1st (junior pairs with Pierre Benoit)
1939 Minto Skating Club Ladies Prize for Skating - 1st (junior)
1940 Canadian Figure Skating Championships - 1st (junior)
1940 Minto Skating Club Ladies Prize for Skating - 1st
1941 Canadian Figure Skating Championships - 2nd
1941 Minto Skating Club Ladies Prize for Skating - 1st
1941 North American Figure Skating Championships - 6th
1942 Canadian Figure Skating Championships - 2nd
1943 Minto Skating Club Ladies Prize for Skating - 1st

1944 Canadian Figure Skating Championships - 1st
1944 Minto Skating Club Ladies Prize for Skating - 1st
1945 North American Figure Skating Championships - 1st
1946 Canadian Figure Skating Championships - 1st
1947 European Figure Skating Championships - 1st
1947 World Figure Skating Championships - 1st
1947 North American Figure Skating Championships - 1st
1948 European Figure Skating Championships - 1st
1948 Winter Olympic Games - 1st
1948 World Figure Skating Championships - 1st
1948 Canadian Figure Skating Championships - 1st

APPENDIX C – ITINERARY OF SKATING SENSATIONS OF 1950 TOUR

1949

Winnipeg, MB - October 10-15 (Winnipeg Amphitheatre)
Vancouver, BC - October 18-20 (Vancouver Forum)
New Westminster, BC - October 21-22 (New Westminster Arena)
Kamloops, BC - October 24-25 (Kamloops Memorial Arena)
Kelowna, BC - October 26-27 (Kelowna Memorial Arena)
Vernon, BC - October 28-29 (Vernon Civic Arena)
Calgary, AB - November 1-5 (Arena Rink)
Edmonton, AB - November 8-12 (Edmonton Gardens)
Lethbridge, AB - November 14-15 (Lethbridge Arena)
Regina, SK - November 17-19 (Regina Exhibition Stadium)
Moose Jaw, SK - November 21-22 (Moose Jaw Stadium)
Saskatoon, SK - November 24-26 (Saskatoon Arena)
Brandon, MB - November 29-30 (Wheat City Arena)
Port Arthur, ON - December 2-3 (Port Arthur Arena)
Sudbury, ON - December 6-7 (Copper Cliff Skating

Club)
Sault Ste. Marie. ON - December 8-10 (Sault Ste. Marie Memorial Gardens)
Wallaceburg, ON - December 12 (Wallaceburg Memorial Arena)
Chatham, ON - December 13-14 (Chatham Memorial Arena)
Windsor, ON - December 15-17 (Windsor Arena)
Sarnia, ON - December 20-22 (Sarnia Arena)

Christmas Vacation – December 22-27

Stratford, ON - December 27-28 (Stratford Arena)
Kitchener, ON - December 29-30 (Waterloo Memorial Arena)

1950

Owen Sound, ON - January 3-4 (Owen Sound Arena)
Guelph, ON - January 5-7 (Guelph Memorial Gardens)
Simcoe, ON - January 9 (Simcoe Arena)
Galt, ON - January 10-11 (Galt Arena Gardens)
Hamilton, ON - January 12-14 (Barton Street Arena)
Belleville, ON - January 16-17 (Hume Arena)
Barrie, ON - January 18-19 (Barrie Arena)
North Bay, ON - January 20-21 (North Bay Memorial Gardens)
Schumacher, ON - January 23-25 (Schumacher Community Building)
Oshawa, ON - January 27-28 (Oshawa Arena)
Cornwall, ON - January 30-31 (Cornwall Community Arena)

Ottawa, ON - February 1-4 (Ottawa Auditorium)
Shawinigan Falls, QC – February 5-6 (L'Aréna Jacques-Plante)
Glace Bay, NS - February 9-11 (Miners' Forum)
Saint John, NB - February 13-15 (Saint John Forum)
St. Andrews by-the-Sea, NB - February 16-18 (St. Andrews Arena)
Fredericton, NB - February 20-22 (York Arena)
Amherst, NS - February 23-25 (Bailey Arena)
Stellarton, NS - February 27-28 (Stellarton Memorial Rink)
Sackville, NB - March 1-2 (Allison Gardens)
Charlottetown, PEI - March 3-4 (Charlottetown Forum)
Granby, QC - March 7-8 (L'Aréna de Granby)
Sherbrooke, QC - March 9-11 (Sherbrooke Arena)
Valleyfield, QC - March 12-13 (Aréna Salaberry)
Troy, NY - March 15-19 ((Field House, Rensselaer Polytechnic Institute)
Clinton, NY - March 20-22 (Clinton Arena)
Welland, ON - March 23-25 (Welland-Crowland Arena)
Tillsonburg, ON - March 27-28 (Kinsmen Memorial Arena)
Brantford, ON - March 29-30 (Arctic Arena)
Fort Erie, ON - March 31-April 1 (Fort Erie Memorial Arena)
Niagara Falls, ON - April 3-5 (Niagara Falls Memorial Arena)
Smith's Falls, ON - April 6-7 (Smith's Falls Memorial Community Centre)
Shawinigan Falls, QC - April 8-9 (L'Aréna Shawinigan)
Halifax, NS - April 12-17 (Halifax Forum)
Moncton, NB - April 18-22 (Stadium Moncton)

Rimouski, QC - April 24-26 (L'Aréna Rimouski)
Chicoutimi, QC - April 28-30 (Colisée de Chicoutimi)

APPENDIX D - GENEALOGY

Barbara Ann Scott King
b. May 9, 1928 - Ottawa, ON
d. September 30, 2012 - Fernandina Beach, Amelia Island, FL

Thomas Van Dyke King
b. March 4, 1924 - Cincinnati, OH
d. November 12, 2015 – Fernandina Beach, Amelia Island, FL
Real Estate Executive and President, Merchandise Mart

BARBARA ANN'S PARENTS

Clyde Rutherford Scott
b. September 2, 1893 - Perth, ON
d. September 4, 1941 - Prescott, ON
Colonel, Military Secretary of National Defense

Mary Purvis Derbyshire Scott
b. August 30, 1892 - Brockville, ON
d. December 11, 1986 - Toronto, ON
Real Estate Executive

BARBARA ANN'S HALF-SIBLINGS

William John 'Jack' Derbyshire MacLaren
b. March 5, 1915 - Brockville, ON
d. October 22, 1998 - Cornwall, ON
RCAF Flying Officer, Chief Pilot of World Wide Aviation Agencies

Mary Chalmers MacLaren Woodcock
b. November 18, 1912 - Brockville, ON
d. Unknown

BARBARA ANN'S GRANDPARENTS

Rev. Dr. Alexander Hugh Scott, M.A. F.R.H.S.
b. April 20, 1853 – Martintown, ON
d. November 14, 1931 - Perth, ON
Minister Emeritus, St. Andrews Presbyterian Church, Author

Agnes Schuyler Greenshields Scott
b. June 1, 1857 - Danville, QC
d. March 23, 1936 - Perth, ON

John Alvin Derbyshire
b. May 21, 1870 - Rideau Lakes, ON
d. January 14, 1951 - Brockville, ON
Mayor of Brockville, Produce and Cheese Merchant

Carolina 'Cassie' Louise Purvis Derbyshire
b. December 8, 1871 - Yonge Mills, ON
d. February 13, 1936 - Brockville, ON

BARBARA ANN'S GREAT GRANDPARENTS

Hon. Daniel Derbyshire
b. December 11, 1846 - Plum Hollow, ON
d. June 18, 1916 - Brockville, ON
Senator, Member of Parliament for Brockville, Mayor of Brockville, Prominent Farmer & Dairy Supplier known as "The Eastern Ontario Cheese King"

Mary Ann (Cauley) Derbyshire
b. November 25, 1847 - Newboyne, ON
d. March 24, 1925 - Brockville, ON

George Arthur Purvis
b. May 28, 1842 - Yonge Mills, ON
d. October 22, 1927 - Leeds, ON
Farmer

Rachael (Rowsom) Purvis
b. October 23, 1843 - Lyn, ON
d. November 24, 1917 - Brockville, ON

William Scott Esq.
b. July 14, 1823 - Alloa, Clackmannanshire, Scotland
d. September 27, 1897 - Martintown, ON
Farmer

Mary (Hamilton) Scott
b. May 1, 1829 - North Branch, ON
d. August 6, 1923 - Martintown, ON

John Greenshields
b. September 18, 1822 - Scotland
d. September 23, 1901 - Iroquois, ON
Livestock Farmer

Margaret (Naismith) Greenshields
b. December 6, 1820 – Scotland
d. May 2, 1900 – Danville, QC

SOURCES

A wide variety of different sources were consulted in the research for this book, including books, newspapers, skating magazines, diaries, scrapbooks, audio and video interviews and archival research. If you'd like to read more about Barbara Ann, consider tracking down the sources below.

The Kingston Whig-Standard, May 4, 1900
The Lanark Era, October 2, 1901
The Ottawa Citizen, June 18, 1910
Canada Census, 1911
The Brantford Weekly Expositor, August 11, 1911
The Ottawa Journal, March 16, 1927
Montreal Gazette, March 21, 1927
The Ottawa Citizen, November 27, 1930
The Ottawa Evening Citizen, May 30, 1935
The Ottawa Journal, March 30, 1936
Skating, Kendall McNeill, May 1936
The Ottawa Journal, March 13, 1937
The Ottawa Citizen, March 15, 1937
The Ottawa Citizen, March 30, 1937
The Ottawa Citizen, March 12, 1938
The Ottawa Journal, March 21, 1938
The Ottawa Citizen, October 29, 1938
Skating, Dorcas G. Griffin, November 1938
The Ottawa Citizen, William Freeman, March 16, 1939
The Ottawa Journal, April 6, 1939
Skating, May 1939
The Ottawa Citizen, September 11, 1939
Skating, October 1939
Scrapbook of figure skating photographs and clippings, 1940s, author's collection, donated by Yvonne Butorac
The Ottawa Journal, January 19, 1940

The Ottawa Citizen, January 20, 1940
The Ottawa Journal, January 20, 1940
The Montreal Gazette, March 26, 1940
The Ottawa Journal, March 30, 1940
Skating, May 1940
The Ottawa Journal, Will McLaughlin, May 4, 1940
Skating, Elizabeth McGee, December 1940
Skating, Madge Austin and Dr. A.E. Broome, October 1940
The Ottawa Journal, January 20, 1941
Waterloo Region Record, January 22, 1941
The Philadelphia Inquirer, Dora Lurie, February 12, 1941
Skating, Kathleen M. Leslie, March 1941
The Montreal Star, July 25, 1941
The Ottawa Journal, September 4, 1941
Skating, April 1942
Skating, Alison Chown, March 1942
Skating, May 1942
The Winnipeg Tribune, June 25, 1942
The Winnipeg Tribune, October 9, 1942
Skating, March 1943
Kingston Whig-Standard, March 22, 1943
The Ottawa Journal, September 28, 1943
Skating, October 1943
The Ottawa Citizen, Winston Mills, February 5, 1944
Skating, Mavis Berry Daane and Naomi Slater Heydon, March 1944
The Ottawa Citizen, March 3, 1944
Skating, December 1944
Programme, Ice Frolics of 1945, Oshawa Skating Club, March 1945
Skating, Theresa Weld Blanchard and Milda Alten, March 1945
The Ottawa Citizen, April 21, 1945
Skating, May 1945
The Ottawa Journal, May 21, 1945
Skating, October 1945
The Kingston Whig-Standard, December 22, 1945
Skating, January 1946
North Bay Nugget, February 8, 1946
Skating, Elizabeth Shields, March 1946
The Ottawa Journal, November 6, 1946

The Standard, Gerald Waring, December 14, 1946
Journals of The House of Commons of the Dominion of Canada, 20th Parliament, 3rd Session: Vol. 88, January 30 to July 17, 1947, Library of Parliament Archives
The Ottawa Journal, January 6, 1947
The Hamilton Spectator, January 9, 1947
Ice Skating, Cyril Beastall, February 1947
Diaries of William Lyon Mackenzie King, February 16, 1947
The Ottawa Citizen, February 17, 1947
The Ottawa Evening Citizen, February 17, 1947
The Vancouver Sun, February 17, 1947
Programme, 1947 North American Figure Skating Championships and Minto Skating Club Revue
Skating World, Nigel Brown and Dr. Cyril F. MacGillicuddy, March 1947
Buffalo Courier-Press Pictorial, March 2, 1947
The Ottawa Evening Citizen, Austin F. Cross, March 3, 1947
The Ottawa Citizen, Otto Gold, March 4, 1947
The Ottawa Evening Citizen, Austin F. Cross, W.M. Gladish and Bettie L. Cole, March 4, 1947
The Toronto Star, Jack Karr, March 6, 1947
The Ottawa Citizen, Alan Harvey, March 6, 1947
The Montreal Star, March 7, 1947
Diaries of William Lyon Mackenzie King, March 7, 1947
The Ottawa Citizen, Cameron Rougvie, March 7, 1947
The Ottawa Evening Citizen, Thomas H. Turner, March 7, 1947
The Montreal Gazette, March 8, 1947
The Ottawa Citizen, March 8, 1947
The Ottawa Citizen, March 9, 1947
The Ottawa Citizen, March 10, 1947
The Toronto Star, March 11, 1947
The Canadian Statesman, March 13, 1947
The Ottawa Citizen, March 13, 1947
The Ottawa Citizen, March 19, 1947
Skating, March 1947
Ice Skating, Cyril Beastall, April 1947
Skating, Lyman E. Wakefield Jr., April 1947
Ottawa Citizen, April 18, 1947

Skating, Donald B. Cruikshank, Ulrich Salchow and Patricia Kennedy, May 1947
The Toronto Star, Alexandrine Gibb, May 6, 1947
The Berkeley Gazette, May 23, 1947
Ice Skating, Cyril Beastall, June 1947
The Ottawa Journal, June 10, 1946
The Montreal Star, June 27, 1947
Diaries of William Lyon Mackenzie King, June 27, 1947
Skating World, July 1947
Diary of Wanda Lefurgey Wyatt, July 14, 1949 to May 14, 1950, McNaught History Centre and Archives
Diaries of William Lyon Mackenzie King, August 22, 1947
Skating World, Walter Farrar, September 1947
Ice Skating, Cyril Beastall, October 1947
Sport, Austin F. Cross, November 1947
The Ottawa Citizen, November 25, 1947
The Ottawa Citizen, November 26, 1947
Programme for Olympic Night Featuring R.C.A.F Flyers, Canadian Olympic Team vs McGill Red Men - Added attraction Barbara Ann Scott, December 1947
The Ottawa Citizen, December 6, 1947
Calgary Herald, December 16, 1947
The Ottawa Citizen, December 16, 1947
Scrapbook of Barbara Ann Scott photographs and clippings, 1948, author's collection, donated by Yvonne Butorac
"She Skated Into Our Hearts", Cay Moore, 1948
Samara 1948 Yearbook, Elmwood School
Letter from Sheldon Galbraith to Donald B. Cruikshank, January 3, 1948
Saint John Times Globe, January 8, 1948
Time, January 26, 1948
Time, February 2, 1948
The Boston Globe, Maribel Vinson Owen, February 6, 1948
Diaries of William Lyon Mackenzie King, February 6, 1948
Interview with Barbara Ann Scott, CBC Radio, Basil Dean, February 6, 1948, CBC Archives
The Montreal Gazette, February 7, 1948
The Montreal Gazette, February 11, 1948

Diaries of William Lyon Mackenzie King, February 16, 1948
Montreal Gazette, February 17, 1948
Moncton Transcript, February 18, 1948
Skating World, Nigel Brown and Harry Hirsch, March 1948
Skating, Theresa Weld Blanchard and Edith E. Ray, March 1948
Diaries of William Lyon Mackenzie King, March 9, 1948
The Ottawa Citizen, March 9, 1948
Dundee Evening Telegraph, March 11, 1948
Skating, Theresa Weld Blanchard, April 1948
Daily Mirror, April 14, 1948
The Ottawa Journal, April 20, 1948
The Evening Telegram, May 5, 1948
The Ottawa Journal, May 17, 1948
Skating, June 1948
Skating World, Nigel Brown, October 1948
Skating, November 1948
Skating, December 1948
Skating World, Harry Hirsch, December 1948
The Evening Telegram, Barbara Ann Scott, December 21, 1948
The Ottawa Citizen, December 27, 1948
Scrapbook of Barbara Ann Scott photographs and clippings, 1949-early 1950s, author's collection, donated by Yvonne Butorac
Skating, John S. MacLean, February 1949
MacLean's, Eva-Lis Wuorio, February 15, 1949
Diaries of Prime Minister William Lyon Mackenzie King, March 4, 1949
Skating, April 1949
Skyways, Noel Bart, Vol. 8, No. 4, April 1949
Toronto Daily Star, April 1, 1949
Chicago Tribune, May 8, 1949
Skating, June 1949
Flash, Walter Clark, September 6, 1949
The Native Voice, Mildred Valley Thornton, Vol. 3, Issue 11, November 1949
Programmes, Skating Sensations of 1950, Fall 1949-Spring 1950
"Skate With Me", Barbara Ann Scott, 1950
Coronet, Harry Henderson and Sam Shaw, January 1950
The Standard, Andy O'Brien, January 7, 1950

Toronto Daily Star, January 11, 1950
Skating World, Cyril Beastall, June 1950
The Ottawa Journal, June 5, 1950
Daily Gleaner, June 3, 1950
Skating, December 1950
The Ottawa Citizen, December 16, 1950
Skating, January 1951
Ottawa Citizen, January 15, 1951
MacLean's, Barbara Ann Scott and Eva-Lis Wuorio, January 15, 1951
Montreal Gazette, February 7, 1951
Daily Standard-Freeholder, February 7, 1951
Saint John Times Globe, February 7, 1951
Herald and News, February 7, 1951
The Star-Ledger, February 8, 1951
The Toronto Star, February 14, 1951
Skating, May 1951
Evening Standard, June 9, 1951
The Ottawa Citizen, August 28, 1951
The Buffalo News, August 28, 1951
The Sun Times, September 28, 1951
Skating World, Dennis L. Bird, October 1951
Weekend, Andy O'Brien, October 13, 1951
Janesville Weekly Gazette, November 6, 1951
The Indianapolis Star, November 14, 1941
Redwood City Tribune, November 23, 1951
Skating World, Martin Holden, December 1951
Chicago Tribune, December 26, 1951
Skating, William C. Firestone, January 1952
Flash, January 19, 1952
Courier-Post, Bud Stretch, January 19, 1952
The Sunday News, January 20, 1952
Staten Island Advance, January 23, 1952
The Vancouver Sun, March 18, 1952
Toronto Daily Star, Milt Dunnel, April 9, 1952
Whitehorse Daily Star, April 18, 1952
The Telegram, April 24, 1952
The Ottawa Journal, May 2, 1952

The Ottawa Citizen, June 3, 1952
The Ottawa Journal, June 7, 1952
The Miami News, July 25, 1952
Skating, Robert Sackett, January 1953
The Boston Globe, January 10, 1953
Skating, Theresa Weld Blanchard, April 1954
Toronto Daily Star, August 30, 1955
Toronto Daily Star, Vancy Gordon, September 19, 1955
The Telegram, September 19, 1955
Daily Times-Gazette, September 19, 1955
Daily Mirror, September 19, 1955
"Dick Button on Skates", Dick Button, 1956
Chicago Tribune, January 1, 1956
The Orlando Sentinel, January 1, 1956
The Ottawa Citizen, Austin F. Cross, August 16, 1956
The Indianapolis Star, October 24, 1956
Star Weekly, Angela Burke, December 1, 1956
Weekend, Vol. 7, No. 33, 195, Robert McKeown, August 17, 1957
Omaha World-Herald, October 20, 1957
"Good Housekeeping's Who's Who Cooks: Favorite Recipes of Famous People", Good Housekeeping, 1958
Skating World, Cyril Beastall, October 1958
"Ice-Skating: A History", Nigel Brown, 1959
The Hamilton Spectator, April 13, 1959
The Kingston Whig-Standard, June 26, 1959
Chatelaine, Dorothy Sangster, September 1959
Weekend Magazine (The Telegram), Andy O'Brien, January 23, 1960
The Ottawa Citizen, July 25, 1960
Press Release, Democratic National Committee, October 29, 1960, John F. Kennedy Presidential Library and Museum
"Scott: An Account of the Families Descended from Alexander Scott, Emigrant of Scotland, with Sketches of the Families, Pioneers and Related Material", Grace L. Hartley, 1961
World Ice Skating Guide, 1961
Encyclopedia of Jews in Sports, Bernard Postal, Jesse and Roy Silver, 1965
Watertown Daily Times, April 23, 1965

Skating, Martha H. Roynon, November 1965
World Ice Skating Guide, 1966
The Leader-Post (Regina), June 14, 1966
Newsweek, February 5, 1968
Chicago Sun Times, Linda Rockey, November 11, 1968
Skating World, January 1969
Skating, Dick Button, June 1971
Skating, Betty Campbell, June 1972
"Canada's Sporting Heroes: Their Lives and Times", S.F. Wise and D. Fisher, 1974
The Toronto Star, April 9, 1977
The Scarborough Mirror, April 13, 1977
Skating, Benjamin T. Wright, February 1980
The Globe and Mail, Deborah King, February 11, 1980
The Ottawa Citizen, Shirley Foley, February 12, 1980
Scrapbook of Barbara Ann Scott and Hollywood Ice Revue clippings donated by Tommy Gorman to Library and Archives Canada, prepared in 1981 by Dale Cameron of the Social and Cultural Archives
"For The Record: Canada's Greatest Women Athletes", David McDonald and Lauren Drewery, 1981
The Globe and Mail, Zena Cherry and Nora McCabe, May 5, 1983
"The Golden Age of Canadian Figure Skating", David Young, 1984
The Globe and Mail, Bill Derby, February 4, 1984
Telegraph-Journal, Vera Ayling, February 8, 1985
The Ottawa Citizen, Dave Brown, August 29, 1986
The Toronto Star, December 13, 1986
Canadian Journal of History of Sport, Don Morrow, Vol. 18, Issue 1, 1987
Toronto Star, Mary Ormsby, September 2, 1987
The Globe and Mail, Beverley Smith, November 2, 1987
The Ottawa Citizen, November 17, 1987
Toronto Star, Jim Proudfoot, February 5, 1988
Toronto Star, Paul Hunter, February 8, 1988
Toronto Star, Ellen Bot, March 3, 1988
The Globe and Mail, September 15, 1988
The Montreal Gazette, Judy Creighton, November 17, 1990
Journal Of Sport History, Stephen R. Wenn, Summer 1991

The Globe and Mail, Trent Frayne, February 1, 1991
Toronto Star, Jim Proudfoot, January 17, 1992
"Reflections on the CFSA: A History of the Canadian Figure Skating Association 1887-1990", Teresa Moore, 1993
Toronto Star, Jim Proudfoot, January 26, 1993
Skating, Michelle Seavey Harvath, January 1994
Edmonton Journal, January 16, 1994
MacLean's, February 14, 1994
Toronto Star, February 22, 1994
The Ottawa Citizen, Shelley Page, February 8, 1996
Edmonton Journal, March 20, 1996
Edmonton Journal, Jeff Holubitsky, March 22, 1996
Skating, Anne Udell, September 1996
Toronto Star, Jim Proudfoot, February 1, 1997
The Upper Canadian, Yvonne Butorac, March/April 1997
The Globe and Mail, Beverley Smith, May 26, 1997
SkateHistory.com, Frances Dafoe, December 1997
Ottawa Citizen, Carol Phillips, January 10, 1998
MacLean's, James Deacon, January 12, 1998
Star-Phoenix, Ken Fidlin, February 9, 1998
Ottawa Citizen, Michael Prentice, May 29, 2000
Interview with Osborne Colson, Greg Hill, May 30, 2002
Ottawa Citizen, Clyde Sanger, December 21, 2002
Audio interview with Belita Jepson-Turner, 2003, Pro Skating Historical Foundation Archive, donated by Bill Unwin and Heather Belbin
Ottawa Citizen, Doug Fischer, May 23, 2003
National Post, Judith Fitzgerald, August 5, 2003
"Minto: Skating Through Time - History of the Minto Skating Club 1904-2004", Janet B. Uren, 2004
Ottawa Citizen, Michael Prentice, May 6, 2004
The Windsor Star, John Sewell, September 24, 2005
Kingston Whig-Standard, Lyndon Little, May 7, 2005
The Ottawa Citizen, Jennifer Campbell, January 19, 2007
Toronto Star, Neil Stevens, January 29, 2008
Ottawa Citizen, Gay Cook, January 30, 2008
National Post, Joe O'Connor, February 1, 2008
Calgary Herald, Allen Cameron, April 13, 2008

The National (CBC), December 10, 2009
Interview with Barbara Ann Scott, Allison Manley, The Manleywoman SkateCast, November 2010
The Globe and Mail, Beverley Smith, May 4, 2009
The Beaver, Barbara Schrodt and Mark Reid, December 2009/January 2010 (Vol. 89, Issue 6)
"Taking The Ice: Success Stories from the World of Figure Skating, PJ Kwong", 2010
Interview with Barbara Ann Scott, Paul Henry, City of Ottawa Archives, Barbara Ann Scott: Come Skate with Me Exhibit, 2012
Interview with Elizabeth Manley and Paul Henry, Olga Zeale, City of Ottawa Archives, Barbara Ann Scott: Come Skate with Me Exhibit, 2012
Ottawa Citizen, Martin Cleary, February 7, 2012
Montreal Gazette, March 10, 2012
Ottawa Citizen, David Reevely, August 10, 2012
The National (CBC), October 1, 2012
Ottawa Citizen, Matthew Pearson, October 1, 2012
Ottawa Citizen, Donald Jackson, October 2, 2012
The Vancouver Sun, Martin Cleary, October 2, 2012
The Globe and Mail, Hayley Mick, October 2, 2012
Interview with PJ Kwong, Skate Guard Blog, March 30, 2013
The Globe and Mail, Beverley Smith, May 7, 2015
Correspondence with Liz Deery, Air Historical Branch, Ministry of Defence, September 1, 2021
"Captain Hooper's Farmhouse: The Battle of Kitchener's Wood, Ypres, April 1915", Perth Historical Society, 2022

APPRECIATION

This book would not have been possible had it not been for Yvonne. A fellow author and figure skating history enthusiast, Yvonne salvaged four massive figure skating scrapbooks from the dustbin at a paper sale in Ontario and generously donated them to me last year. Those beautiful scrapbooks were filled with hundreds of 1940s and 1950s newspaper and magazine clippings and photos of Barbara Ann, and without them, I simply couldn't have tackled the gargantuan task of telling her story.

I cannot thank my editor Andrea enough for her care, attention to detail and careful but meaningful revisions. I am also indebted to my BETA readers, Anne, Flynn, Jex, Gila, Tristan, and Mel for your feedback and insightful suggestions on how my early drafts could be improved. I also can't thank my enthusiastic ARC Reader team enough! Like it or lump it, social proof is part of the writing game and I greatly appreciate you taking the time to share your honest opinions on popular book review sites.

To the always fabulous Debbi Wilkes - your generosity and contributions to this project were tremendous – thank you!

The wonderful black-and-white photographs you see only enhance the book. A very special thank you to

Skate Canada/Patinage Canada, the Bibliothèque et Archives nationales du Québec, Toronto Public Library, City of Toronto Archives, Cloyne and District Historical Society, Boston Public Library and the Leslie Jones Collection for your collaboration and support of this project.

AUTHOR'S NOTE

I genuinely hope that you have enjoyed reading **Barbara Ann Scott: Queen of the Ice** as much as I enjoyed researching and writing it.

I have to ask for a small favour though. Could you please spare a few minutes to write a brief review on the retailer's website and popular book review platforms? Reviews play a critical role in the success of all books, but they hold even greater importance for independently published ones.

I would also be extremely appreciative if you could visit your local library's website and fill out a short 'Suggest a Purchase' form.

I am grateful for your kind support in helping this important history reach the hands of more people!

BOOKS BY THIS AUTHOR

Barbara Ann Scott: Queen of the Ice

Sequins, Scandals & Salchows: Figure Skating in the 1980s

Jackson Haines: The Skating King

Technical Merit: A History of Figure Skating Jumps

A Bibliography of Figure Skating

The Almanac of Canadian Figure Skating

www.ingramcontent.com/pod-product-compliance
Lightning Source LLC
LaVergne TN
LVHW051518070426
835507LV00023B/3184